T0305465

University Entrepreneurial Ecosystems

University Entrepreneurial Ecosystems

Spinouts, Networks and Geography

Daniel Prokop

Senior Lecturer in Economic Geography, School of Geography and Planning, Cardiff University, UK

Edward Elgar PUBLISHING

Cheltenham, UK • Northampton, MA, USA

Published by
Edward Elgar Publishing Limited
The Lypiatts
15 Lansdown Road
Cheltenham
Glos GL50 2JA
UK

Edward Elgar Publishing, Inc.
William Pratt House
9 Dewey Court
Northampton
Massachusetts 01060
USA

A catalogue record for this book
is available from the British Library

Library of Congress Control Number: 2024941731

This book is available electronically in the **Elgar**online
Geography, Planning and Tourism subject collection
https://dx.doi.org/10.4337/9781803924755

ISBN 978 1 80392 474 8 (cased)
ISBN 978 1 80392 475 5 (eBook)

Printed and bound by CPI Group (UK) Ltd, Croydon, CR0 4YY

Contents

Figures

Tables

Acknowledgements

This book was an intensive project, completion of which would have not been possible without my wife Saloomeh, thank you!

1. Introduction to *University Entrepreneurial Ecosystems*

The increasing attention drawn in recent years to the concept of entrepreneurial ecosystems (Alvedalen and Boschma 2017; Malecki 2018; Wurth et al. 2022) has enabled developments in understanding how entrepreneurship develops in places, which actors are important to the functioning of the ecosystems and finally how these ecosystem constructs help us understand place-based economic development (Huggins et al. 2024). The concept represents the current stage of evolution of thinking that emerged from clusters (Porter 1990), national systems of innovation (Lundvall 1992), regional systems of innovation (Cooke 1992), triple helix (Etzkowitz and Leydesdorff 1995), learning regions (Storper 1993; Florida 1995; Asheim 1996; Morgan 1997), and others. What it leads us to understand is that geography matters (Audretsch and Feldman 1996), not least because certain cities/towns, regions or nations perform better than others, but also in recognising that the complexity of the spatial circumstances of a place or region can explain the development of economic activities (Gallup et al. 1999), their sectoral composition (Davis and Weinstein 1999), the type of relations formed and exercised between actors (Ter Wal and Boschma 2009; Maggioni and Uberti 2011), the entrepreneurial rates, growth and survival (Sternberg 2022; Plummer and Pe'er 2010), and most importantly, the economic development outcomes of places (Audretsch 2018; Krugman 1999).

As such, firms that are characterised by high levels of innovation and growth draw scholarly and policy attention through the ecosystem metaphor (Mason and Brown 2014), as these are posited to disrupt the markets and have a larger local economic impact, not least through increased levels of employment across workforce with tertiary education. Such firms are more likely to be identified closer to key sources of basic knowledge – the universities. This pronounced importance of high technology and high-growth firms keeps policymakers interested in academic spinouts in the UK (e.g. Lambert Review (2003), Independent Review of Spinout Companies (Tracey and Williamson 2023)), the US (e.g. The Green Book (FLC 2018), Italy (e.g. OECD/EU 2019) and elsewhere, with their potential for substantial contribution to economic development.

Academic spinouts are firms based on research conducted by university staff, at the moment of firm foundation typically owned by the universities and staff, making them unique, in that they commercialise knowledge that is often decades away from the technological paradigm of consumer markets, transferring radically innovative solutions and achieving higher levels of survival (Prokop et al. 2019). What further distinguishes them from typical start-ups or corporate spin-offs is that their founders have limited if any commercial background, making them critically reliant on the university entrepreneurial ecosystem for support to develop the company and its underlying technology.

The motivation behind this book is in developing and capitalising on the emerging debates that began to link academic spinouts to entrepreneurial ecosystems (Hayter et al. 2018), by focusing on their asymmetric opportunities. The evidence of this is drawn from recent general ecosystems literature identifying spatial inequalities of outcomes (Vedula and Kim 2019), increasingly centred on the role of universities (Heaton et al. 2019), and drawing on the network-based view (Scott et al. 2021). Specifically, this book advances the literature by comprehensively analysing the notion of university entrepreneurial ecosystems, their relational and spatial character, and explaining their variable performance.

This theoretical complexity requires careful unpacking, as much of the literature on entrepreneurial ecosystems shows (e.g. Alvedalen and Boschma 2017; Wurth et al. 2022) that the concept remains undertheorised, understudied and potentially misunderstood as a result (Stam 2015). Whilst there have been very good attempts to theorise entrepreneurial ecosystems, these efforts have not exhausted many fundamental questions about how ecosystems function, how they are organised, bounded and configured, or how each ecosystem relates to each other.

As such, the purpose of this book is to try and systematically resolve these problems. By developing the concept of university entrepreneurial ecosystems, adding theoretical delineations derived from network theory and spatial perspectives, the book contributes to three key streams of literature, namely academic entrepreneurship, entrepreneurial ecosystems and economic geography. Specifically, the book builds on the still developing geography of ecosystems literature, and how the locational aspects explain divergent performance of ecosystems. Furthermore, as the literature typically focuses on the examples of large cities, the book adds to the literature by recognising that university entrepreneurial ecosystems exist in towns and peripheral regions, and draws attention of the readers to their challenges.

Additionally, the book employs a network-based view, which follows connections between actors without assuming spatial boundaries. It builds on the ecosystems literature that sought network explanations, but lacked connection to geography. Consequently, it contributes to the extant research by recognising and theorising the links made by university entrepreneurial ecosystem actors and defining the boundaries of ecosystems.

The book engages with the literatures on academic spinouts, industrial organisation, university knowledge generation, university–industry links, knowledge spillover theory of entrepreneurship, regional studies, firm relocation and social network theory. As such, it offers a contribution through the unique combination of theoretical inputs from distinct and often isolated bodies of work, pulling together multiple conceptual strands to offer improved theoretical clarity in order to move the field and thinking on university entrepreneurial ecosystems (and ecosystems more broadly) forward. This is especially critical, as the ecosystems research is rich and vibrant, yet fragmented, struggling with the conceptual issues (Audretsch et al. 2019), and in need of a novel perspective.

This book does not resolve all theoretical and empirical problems of university entrepreneurial ecosystems; however, its focus is to add to theorising of university entrepreneurial ecosystems concept by considering the perspectives that have either been largely omitted or underutilised in ecosystems research. This is not only because university entrepreneurial ecosystems are important and unique ecosystems to understand (as the following chapters show), but also because by drawing our attention to university entrepreneurial ecosystems many theoretical problems originating from the wider entrepreneurial ecosystems literature become more visible. As such, the research gaps become more transparent, and this opens up the possibility of explaining them by building university entrepreneurial ecosystems theory.

At this point, one may ask, who is this book for? Whilst primarily it is aimed at fellow students of university entrepreneurial ecosystems and entrepreneurial ecosystems more generally, it will assist local, regional and central policymakers in making sense of the concept, not least because the following chapters may explain how different university entrepreneurial ecosystems coexist and relate to each other, or where we should draw the theoretical boundaries. The book is also aimed at a wider audience of stakeholders or actors of the university entrepreneurial ecosystems, in part to understand how they fit in, but also to understand how what they form functions, and how best to utilise this understanding to improve their ecosystem roles. Finally, and most importantly, it is aimed at universities and their administrators to understand that the role they play is critical, and cross-cutting through different scales and types of ecosystems, enabling them to hopefully reflect on how they engage in ecosystems, and what meaningful strategies they could pursue to maximise the returns to university and to the university entrepreneurial ecosystem they are part of.

WHY DO UNIVERSITY ENTREPRENEURIAL ECOSYSTEMS MATTER?

There are multiple definitions of entrepreneurial ecosystems (e.g. Mason and Brown 2014; Stam 2015; Spigel 2017; Brown and Mason 2017), highlighting the interdependency of actors, the institutional and cultural attributes, naming some of the key actors as entrepreneurs, universities, finance providers and stressing self-organised or coalescing co-ordination of activities, resulting in productive entrepreneurship that contributes to ecosystem's economic development. As recognised in the literature (e.g. Stam 2015; Brown and Mason 2017), many of the properties of the entrepreneurial ecosystems have been well known in the literatures on entrepreneurship and economic geography, e.g. Marshall's localisation economies or Jacob's urbanisation economies, yet the literature did not necessarily have a single framework that had theoretical space for all these concepts.

Whilst understanding what an entrepreneurial ecosystem is has been an important early endeavour in the literature, equally important, yet only recent, is the theorisation of the ecosystem's development. The emergence of the entrepreneurial ecosystem is characterised by a level of coherence in actions taken by ecosystem actors (Roundy et al. 2018). This coherence is not imposed on them, but rather develops gradually and organically or in reaction to events (Cloutier and Messeghem 2022), such as policies (Nordling 2019), as an aggregate of individual interactions (Roundy et al. 2018). At this initial stage it is also important to observe the development of some of the key actors, such as finance and support organisations, but also increasing entrepreneurial activity (Mack and Mayer 2016). Interestingly, migrants and transnational entrepreneurs have been recognised as potentially playing a role in these emergent processes by contributing human capital, resources, or entrepreneurial activity (Schäfer and Henn 2018). These growing numbers of studies are clearly uncovering a complex picture.

It is notable to observe that the emergence of entrepreneurial ecosystems is strongly dependent on the network activity (Roundy et al. 2018; Haarhaus et al. 2020; Scott et al. 2021), even if not expressed explicitly: the formation of ties, the development of actions based on the homophilious character of connections formed (where such homophily could be based on any number and combination of attributes – education, ethnicity, sector, occupation, views, norms, etc.), the emergence of network characteristics such as centrality and relatedly network roles, e.g. brokerage – performed by dealmakers (Feldman and Zoller 2016). Critically, it is not the mere presence of networks that is important, but what each tie is employed for (Clifton et al. 2020).

Further growth of entrepreneurial ecosystems is a result of the increasingly coherent activity of an ecosystem's elements or actors (Mack and Mayer 2016), manifested by an increase in successful enterprises that may act as champions for the ecosystem's new and potential entrepreneurs, or sources of human and entrepreneurial capital (Spigel and Vinodrai 2021). These changes would normally be accompanied by greater availability of finance, the development of human capital (for example, from the successful ventures), entrepreneurial recycling and the emergence and densification of support organisations, but also, consequently the densification of networks. Unlike in emergent or nascent ecosystems, where resources may have been leaking outside of the ecosystem, this stage shows increasing attraction of resources into the ecosystem (Spigel and Harrison 2018). As such the growth stage may also be characterised by a transition in governance format of the entrepreneurial ecosystems, from a more hierarchical one to one based on relational organisation (Colombelli et al. 2019).

At the maturity stage entrepreneurial ecosystems become more established, with firm births continuing to outstrip the firm deaths, whilst resources such as finance and network or human capital begin to decline in availability (Mack and Mayer 2016). Cantner et al. (2021) suggest that at this point in the entrepreneurial ecosystem development entrepreneurship activity reaches parity with intrapreneurship activity, suggesting a potential to transition either towards a business ecosystem or towards finding a new path of growth as entrepreneurial ecosystem. At this point in the entrepreneurial ecosystem its networks become widely developed and densely connected (Colombelli et al. 2019); however, they may suffer from rigidity (Auerswald and Dani 2017), potentially expressed in lock-in or homophily. This inability to change or introduce new diverse connections may hinder further development of the ecosystem and/or its resilience (Roundy 2017). The self-organisation of the ecosystem is self-reinforcing as a consequence of cultural and institutional developments (Colombelli et al. 2019).

Transitioning from the maturity stage leads entrepreneurial ecosystems towards three key potential evolutionary trajectories: decline, renewal and sustainability. Ecosystems that suffer from network lock-in or limited connections with diverse actors, where culture and institutions may no longer support entrepreneurship activity, may enter a path of decline (Mack and Mayer 2016). In a critique of evolutionary models presenting decline as the only final development path Malecki (2018) suggests that more positive outcomes should not be discounted. Strong evidence for this can be found in the clusters literature (e.g. Huggins 2008), suggesting a clear possibility (and examples) of renewal, e.g. continuously manifested in Silicon Valley. These positive development paths may be a result of the non-linear dynamics of the entrepreneurial ecosystems, where multiple actors, different levels and elements of an ecosystem may operate at different speeds and across different timeframes (Roundy et al. 2018). When entrepreneurial ecosystems continue to generate new productive ventures, their networks continue to strengthen, there is a clear activity of serial entrepreneurs and the support structures and resources remain accessible and available, they may enter onto a self-sustainable path (Cukier et al. 2015). The renewal or reorganisation phase is characterised by reconfiguration of networks, declining density, with many established connections ceasing and the emergence of new ties, spurring the emergence of a new path, new industries and/or new technologies (Auerswald and Dani 2017).

These definitions and evolutionary explanations do not delineate an ecosystem: specifically, where the conceptual boundary should stop and whether it is a spatial boundary, sectoral, or organisational, even when such concerns were clearly articulated (Stam 2015). As such a growing literature appears to focus on ecosystems of business incubators (Van Rijnsoever 2020; Theodoraki 2020), specific sectoral ecosystems (e.g. fintech) (Berman et al. 2022), but also local or regional ecosystems (Rocha et al. 2021; Bichler et al. 2022). Furthermore, one needs to ask if a very specific entrepreneurial ecosystem, built around an anchor tenant such as a university, that for a number of very good reasons, e.g. public funding, cannot cease to exist, can ever decline. Specifically, how would that look like in terms of theoretical models of their evolution, with some universities present for hundreds of years, strongly embedded within their localities, with long histories of generating academic spinouts (Shane 2004). To what extent is it possible to identify the emergence of university entrepreneurial ecosystems? If the literature has studied all-sectoral entrepreneurial ecosystems and single-sector ecosystems, as well as university entrepreneurial ecosystems, there is a possibility that one sub-ecosystem declines, but the wider all-sectoral or generic entrepreneurial ecosystem of a place remains stable (or vice versa).

The university entrepreneurial ecosystems have gained less attention, yet the developing literature on them shows their critical position within the ecosystems debates (Miller and Acs 2017; Theodoraki et al. 2018; Secundo et al. 2021; Prokop 2021, 2022). The uniqueness of the university entrepreneurial ecosystems is two-fold: (a) as ecosystem concepts – they cross-cut through all types of ecosystems highlighted above, and as this book will show, this is largely thanks to the strong role of the key university entrepreneurial ecosystem actor, i.e. the university, its local and regional embeddedness (Bramwell and Wolfe 2008) and national and international connectedness (Collins 2012); and (b) as key engines of regional economic development, illustrated by a wealth of literature in innovation, entrepreneurship and regional studies (Goldstein and Renault 2004; Drucker and Goldstein 2007; Motoyama and Mayer 2017), not least where such ecosystems connect with local, regional and national entrepreneurial ecosystem actors, but also by contributing ideas, knowledge, human capital, networks and very successful high technology ventures – academic spinouts (Prokop et al. 2019) – to their respective economies.

Universities are unique anchor tenants in entrepreneurial ecosystems. As institutions that in many countries are publicly funded, their survival is rarely threatened, enabling them to act as some of the most stable actors. Unlike large firms posing as anchor tenants, universities generate large volumes of highly diversified human capital talent released every year to the local, regional, national and even international labour pools. In addition to that, universities generate knowledge and engage in its transfer with local and non-local businesses (e.g. Huggins et al. 2010) or by collaborating with the most R&D-intensive firms (Huggins et al. 2016), which act as anchor tenants in their respective ecosystems. In fact, universities do even more, they establish their own high technology ventures based on the latest university-generated knowledge (Prokop 2023) that many firms themselves would be unable to either absorb (Cohen and Levinthal 1990) or utilise productively. This knowledge, if not commercially developed by universities, could have lost its potential to benefit the society at large, or could have been developed independently by non-academic entrepreneurs at a much later date. This is especially visible in the discrepancy between the technological advancement of university research and the current technological paradigm of what markets can absorb (Prokop 2017). It is often manifested in the fact that not all knowledge of university origin is considered of commercialisable value, as some of its benefits are not yet understood.

As such, the universities could be considered as repositories of knowledge that have potential to feed local and/or regional high technology entrepreneurial activity, and consequently, the university entrepreneurial ecosystems and their wider local or regional entrepreneurial ecosystems. This positions university entrepreneurial ecosystems as critical environments that generate productive entrepreneurship (Mason and Brown 2014). In fact, the success of the ventures generated by universities often outpaces that of regular enterprises (Bonardo et al. 2011).

Whilst only a few unique characteristics of the university entrepreneurial ecosystems have been considered in this introduction, they paint a picture of an ecosystem that is highly economically relevant, spatially embedded, and crucially, it is important to explore, theorise and highlight their role in stimulating entrepreneurial activity. This will become even more evident from the next chapters that depict university entrepreneurial ecosystems in greater detail.

THE CONCEPTUAL CHALLENGES

As unique types of ecosystems, university entrepreneurial ecosystems pose multiple theoretical challenges that this book aims to address. In doing so, the book builds on the concept by resolving ambiguities that stem from limited attention devoted to the existence of multiple types of entrepreneurial ecosystems, and especially, one type that questions the state of knowledge on entrepreneurial ecosystems, namely the university entrepreneurial ecosystems. The result is a more systematised state of knowledge on university (and) entrepreneurial ecosystems, their organisation, function and success.

In deriving these challenges, the book draws on insights from network and spatial perspectives, which have not played a substantial enough role in the emerging literature on entrepreneurial ecosystems, as presented in critiques from Alvedalen and Boschma (2017) or Malecki (2018).

The key challenge of this work is to understand why university entrepreneurial ecosystems produce asymmetric opportunities. Whilst much of the literature tends to focus on studying individual ecosystems, the configuration and locational circumstances of each individual university entrepreneurial ecosystem result in different outcomes (Prokop 2021). This is a grand challenge, as the entrepreneurial ecosystem literature recognises the characteristics that may lead to different outcomes (e.g. Stam 2015), but these are difficult to apply to university entrepreneurial ecosystems, where within a single location two such ecosystems may co-exist, potentially bounded by similar institutional and cultural parameters, key dimensions used to explain some of these differences.

The remaining challenges break down the focus of the underlying aim of this book into specific research questions that will be explored in the subsequent chapters. Whilst the literature on university entrepreneurial ecosystems has been gaining some ground (e.g. Miller and Acs 2017; Hayter et al. 2018; Theodoraki et al. 2018; Secundo et al. 2021; Prokop 2021, 2022), a clear delineation is required to define what these are and why we should refer to them differently. As such this book answers the following research question: (a) what are university entrepreneurial ecosystems?

Having a clearly delineated university entrepreneurial ecosystem helps with the next challenge partly highlighted in Prokop (2021). The configuration of the university entrepreneurial ecosystems may be very complex and idiosyncratic. It is crucial to understand their compositions and how they co-exist in a single location or different places, when in many instances they are sharing ecosystem elements/ actors. Consequently, an answer is sought here to the subsequent research question: (b) how are university entrepreneurial ecosystems structured and related to each other?

By acknowledging the co-existence of university entrepreneurial ecosystems in a single place, where they may share actors such as investors, accelerators, incubators and business support organisations, a difficulty emerges in understanding why two ecosystems, not just located in different geographies, but in a single place, may generate different outcomes. Some early indication of this problem was presented in Prokop (2022); however, a more comprehensive understanding is required beyond inspecting the ecosystem composition. As a result, the book asks: (c) why do university entrepreneurial ecosystems perform differently?

Given the variable performance of university entrepreneurial ecosystems, it is important to understand what the ecosystems characterised by poorer outcomes should consider in order to improve. This is especially critical, as lower entrepreneurial rates and/or limited quality of local entrepreneurship may have negative influence on economic development of places. As such, university entrepreneurial ecosystem stakeholders, including policymakers across different spatial and administrative scales, may be interested in the following research question: (d) what explains the success of university entrepreneurial ecosystems?

The growing literature on entrepreneurial ecosystems treats these structures as closed systems (e.g. Spigel 2017; Rocha et al. 2021), suggesting that for an ecosystem to be considered one all actors and elements need to be spatially bounded to a single place or region. Early empirical evidence on university entrepreneurial ecosystems (Prokop 2021) suggests that this is not necessarily the case, and in their theorising Spigel and Harrison (2018) acknowledge a rather reduced picture that ecosystems may have outside connections. If such connections exist, they pose a challenge to the spatial understanding of ecosystems, whether these connections are treated as external to the ecosystem or whether the ecosystem should not be regarded as a place-based system, with its configuration being perhaps spatially more dispersed and complex. Consequently, the book pursues the following question: (e) are university entrepreneurial ecosystems closed systems?

Finally, by recognising that the architecture of university entrepreneurial ecosystems may show more spatial complexity, resulting from their network structure (Prokop and Thompson 2023), it is important to draw attention to a very important geographical question, which has great implications for policymaking communities, not least in measuring ecosystems or designing support programmes based on such measures: (f) what are the boundaries of the university entrepreneurial ecosystems? Whilst Schäfer's (2021) work highlighted this issue, a comprehensive and structured answer has not emerged yet in the literature.

The following section outlines how these challenges will be addressed by offering a short insight into each of the remaining nine chapters of the book.

HOW CAN THIS BOOK ADDRESS THE CHALLENGES?

The university's knowledge commercialisation activity is represented through a multitude of channels, inclusive of licensing, consultancy, contract research and academic spinout company formation. Chapter 2 discusses how academic spinout companies are formed, why they are formed and how they develop. In so doing, it highlights their distinctive character drawing exceptional scholarly attention to spinouts: namely, non-commercial background of the founders, its technology based on the latest university research, ability to attract venture capital finance early on and high levels of survival, separating them from typical firms. Through such state-of-the art review, the chapter positions the academic spinout company in the regional economic development processes, specifically examining the current knowledge on the extent of their impact. It introduces the university entrepreneurial ecosystems concept as a lens that enables studying and explaining academic spinout companies, by positioning their existence in complex networks of actors, such as investors, experienced management talent and business incubators.

Universities are often thought of as features of urban areas, yet some higher education institutions are also based in small towns, some of which are located in predominantly rural areas. As such, Chapter 3 aims to explain how universities approach spinout company formation, what makes them decide which knowledge type has entrepreneurial potential, and where spinout companies incubate once established. It is found that universities pursue different formation approaches, some of which include the engagement of venture capitalists at the disclosure stage to identify the most prominent spinout projects and transfer their development to an experienced commercial team. The chapter progresses to challenge the notion that universities, and subsequently their entrepreneurial ecosystems, are merely urban in character, by empirically examining English university entrepreneurial ecosystems with a pronounced rural character that are also responsible for forming spinout companies. It explores the challenges faced by such firms and their university entrepreneurial ecosystems as opposed to their urban based counterparts.

University entrepreneurial ecosystems are characterised by a specific set of actors that support academic spinout company identification, formation, growth and survival. Chapter 4 explores what is known about each of the actors, including universities, technology transfer offices, spinout companies, academic staff, students, science parks and business incubators, external management talent and investors. Specifically, the chapter examines how these actors interact with each other, when they become important in the lifecycle of the spinout company and where they are located. These actors form diverse types of networks that serve spinouts and evolve together with them, specifically pointing towards actors that play early stage roles, such as technology transfer officers, academic staff and universities, and later stage roles involving predominantly external management talent and investors. As such, the chapter builds an evolving model of the university entrepreneurial ecosystem from a spinout company perspective, changing its composition and configuration with phases of spinout company development.

The distinctive character of university entrepreneurial ecosystems suggests that ecosystems not only co-exist across places, but also within them. This importantly presents a conceptual problem, where ecosystems were typically considered as encompassing a specific locality, as singular constructs. The complexity uncovered in Chapter 5 points to a different reality, where a place-based entrepreneurial ecosystem is composed of multiple sub-ecosystems, such as university ones. Consequently, the chapter aims to systematise this by offering a taxonomy of ecosystems, which aims to position and explain the unique existence of university entrepreneurial ecosystems and recognise that other distinctive sub-ecosystems may also be present, such as technology- or sector-based. It then explores how these coexist by proposing alternative explanations through three models: hierarchical, nested and hybrid.

The success of spinout companies is linked to their university entrepreneurial ecosystems, as a result it requires a conceptual model that captures the ecosystem's role. Chapter 6 first examines the knowledge spillover theory of entrepreneurship, leading towards the knowledge filter and observing a gap in explaining the post-start-up success. Drawing on the university entrepreneurial ecosystems concept the chapter proposes an entrepreneurial filter theory. It explains how the theory captures the dynamics of the university entrepreneurial ecosystems and how the ecosystem actors perform a filtration role that determines spinout company's success. Finally, the chapter applies the theory to the general ecosystems concept and the non-spinout firm to present its broader appeal.

Acknowledging the co-existence of sub-ecosystems suggests that the average performance of an overall local ecosystem may hide significant differences between sub-ecosystems. By focusing on the university entrepreneurial ecosystems Chapter 7 explores how and why ecosystems differ, even when their locational conditions appear the same. The empirical part of the chapter specifically observes differences between co-located university entrepreneurial ecosystems and across ecosystems. This approach is employed across two performance measures: academic spinout formation and academic spinout survival. The chapter concludes by developing a conceptual model explaining university entrepreneurial ecosystem performance.

Academic spinout companies are typically portrayed as place-bounded actors, yet emerging evidence suggests a more complex reality. In view of university entrepreneurial ecosystems, Chapter 8 aims to investigate the location patterns of academic spinout companies. In so doing, the chapter maps out spinout companies and their direction of migration across UK regions. It further examines the push and pull factors that help explain why spinout companies move away from their universities. The findings suggest that the relocation activity cannot be explained by the presence of markets for entrepreneurial finance alone. In conclusion, the chapter discusses the 'leakiness' of ecosystems and its consequences for the regional economic development, including the missed direct economic impacts primarily characterised in unrealised local employment and spending, and a development of indirect benefits such as cross-regional networks.

As the actors in university entrepreneurial ecosystems form networks that are not only intra-regional but also inter-regional, it is critical to address this undertheorised space. Specifically, Chapter 9 begins with stating the conceptual problems arising from the current closed-boundaries model of entrepreneurial ecosystems. It discusses what boundaries the ecosystems may exhibit, in particular, by observing the composition and configuration of university entrepreneurial ecosystems. The chapter proposes a taxonomy of ecosystem boundaries and illuminates the methodological issues for ecosystems research. The conclusion offers policy implications, especially aimed at local and central policymakers with a pledge to recognise that in designing policy interventions a more flexible understanding of the ecosystems should be applied.

The final chapter, Chapter 10, summarises the discussions, empirical findings and theoretical models proposed over the course of the book. It highlights that the need to understand the spatial aspects of university entrepreneurial ecosystems is rooted in the asymmetric opportunities available to academic spinout companies across ecosystems, and more generally for all firms situated within any sub- or ecosystem. By recognising this asymmetry the chapter develops a number of recommendations to address them. It concludes by outlining an agenda for future research.

2. Academic entrepreneurship and regional economic development

The aim of this chapter is to show how important academic entrepreneurship activity is to regional economic development. It starts by discussing the nature of academic entrepreneurship, defining academic spinout and outlining why these are unique firms, specifically focusing on the theoretical developments in academic entrepreneurship and regional economic development debates. Subsequently, the chapter introduces the concept of university entrepreneurial ecosystem and explains how it fits within these debates, specifically highlighting the role of university – its key actor.

WHAT IS ACADEMIC ENTREPRENEURSHIP?

With the recognition and more articulated pursuit of Third Mission by universities (Etzkowitz and Leydesdorff 2000), technology transfer became prominently studied in innovation literature, highlighting the important role of universities having a wider remit than just teaching and research. Universities act as employers for the local labour force, as consumers of products and services from local or regional firms, as institutions increasing skills and knowledge of the regional, national and global labour force, as generators of knowledge, and as brokers engaging in entrepreneurial activities. University technology transfer embraces various forms of knowledge diffusion, e.g. patenting, licensing, contract research, consultancy and academic entrepreneurship (Alexander and Martin 2013). Whilst Third Mission is broader than just technology transfer, as it focuses on the universities' role in contributing to the economy and society (Compagnucci and Spigarelli 2020), technology transfer is its most prominent facet.

Academic entrepreneurship has been characterised by the greatest attention devoted to it in the literature, given that it encapsulates all entrepreneurial activities of the academic staff of the university (Fini et al. 2010). This is important at two levels. First, universities, being institutions where knowledge is generated and shared, are not typically considered to engage more directly in entrepreneurship, but rather, at some stage, training and releasing talent that may generate entrepreneurial activity in the future. Second, academic staff, who either lack private industry experience or do not reflect financial motivations, reveal an interesting propensity to not only create firms that exploit their expertise (e.g. consultancies), but to also form companies that prevent the impactful knowledge they generate from being shelved. These companies are widely referred to as academic spinouts.

What is particularly distinctive about universities generating academic spinout companies is that they engage in all three missions of universities: teaching, research and impact (Landry et al. 2006). In other words, not all universities are capable of generating spinout companies, as these require underlying advanced level intellectual property that teaching-oriented institutions typically do not generate at all or in sufficient volumes. As with the second mission of universities – research – there is a synergistic benefit stemming from universities performing more than just teaching (Zawdie 2010), in that the pursuit of multiple missions strengthens each one of them.

WHAT IS AN ACADEMIC SPINOUT?

Since 1980's Bayh–Dole Act US universities have been allowed to retain the intellectual property generated by their staff (Grimaldi et al. 2011), with other countries, including the UK, implementing a similar approach. In essence, this shift in intellectual property ownership is linked to increase in universities' pursuit of knowledge commercialisation (Shane 2004), largely focused on creating companies tasked with translating academic research into innovation. This translation activity is a challenging task, owing to the typically basic nature of academic research, not aimed at commercial markets or solving any practical problems of the day. Such knowledge may not have an immediate commercial value, but could present potential for commercial application. When this commercial potential is recognised, a disclosure is recorded – signifying that a particular piece of knowledge, e.g. new material, could find commercial uses. Disclosure levels are found to be positively related to university departmental culture of technology transfer, but also to higher levels of faculty publishing activity (Bercovitz and Feldman 2008). With further evaluation of this a university may decide what to do with such knowledge, exploring a range of technology transfer routes, before committing to the most complex one in the form of an academic spinout company.

This complexity stems from the nature of knowledge. Understanding new and advanced knowledge carries a tacit character (Nonaka 1991, 1994), consequently being limited to the academics who created it. As knowledge transfer requires both a transmitting party and a receiving one, when the receiving party lacks sufficient absorptive capacity (Cohen and Levinthal 1990), the risk to successful transfer increases. Academic spinout companies resolve this problematic equation by engaging academic staff responsible for the disclosure in such companies, in effect acting as both transmitters and receivers. These academic founders play boundary spanning roles between universities and the private sector (Prokop 2023).

There has been a significant interest in academic spinouts, both at the policy level in terms of assessing the outputs of commercialisation activities (e.g. Lambert 2003), and from industry and academia expressed through external/ privately operating technology transfer offices (Jain and George 2007), proof of concept centres in the US that strengthen the process of building successful companies (Bradley et al. 2013) or the emergence of venture capital companies that focus solely on academic spinouts (e.g. IP Group in the UK). These developments taken together paint a very unique picture of extremely high levels of attention drawn to a very small portion of ventures generated within any region or nation (Prokop and Kitagawa 2022), suggesting that these companies possess unique characteristics that predefine their high levels of success (Prokop et al. 2019) and resulting contribution to local and regional economic development (Vincett 2010).

WHAT MAKES ACADEMIC SPINOUTS DIFFERENT?

The formation of academic spinout companies is far from guaranteed, given the fact that not all academic staff, even if they generate knowledge of commercial potential, may engage in knowledge transfer. It is often found that publishing (Haeussler and Colyvas 2011; Bourelos et al. 2012), academic seniority (Krabel et al. 2012; Clarysse, Tartari and Salter 2011), scientific breadth (D'Este et al. 2012) and research experience (Landry et al. 2006) are correlated with academic entrepreneurship. As such, junior academics that just began their careers with universities are less likely to create spinout companies, instead being focused on developing their teaching and research that in the future, as their careers advance, may lead to academic spinouts. Entrepreneurial intentions of academic staff are typically determined by perceived role models (Prodan and Drnovsek 2010), personal networks (Aldridge and Audretsch 2011), in particular with industry (Goethner et al. 2012), the production of patents (Krabel and Mueller 2009) – signifying the importance of intellectual protection of already codified knowledge and found important in raising startup capital (Clarysse et al. 2007) – and the applied nature of their research (Abreu and Grinevich 2013).

Furthermore, extant research indicates that academic entrepreneurship is typically commenced by 'star scientists' (Vohora et al. 2004; Toole and Czarnitzki 2007; Lawton Smith et al. 2008), who are the most likely to generate research of commercial potential and attract necessary venture funding. The picture drawn presents a very specific successful professor who typically resides in a 'patent-friendly' field, e.g. biotechnology (Shane 2004). Whilst this is the most likely type indicated by studies that predominantly focus on traditional science fields, science bias is not found to be related to the formation of academic spinouts (Prokop and Thompson 2023), suggesting that a wider spectrum of academic staff become entrepreneurs. Whilst science bias was highlighted in a number of studies (Shane 2004; Gubitta et al. 2016), this was typically because these studies were not field agnostic, and frequently focused solely on studying spinouts from traditional science fields (e.g. Vincett 2010).

Given the complexity of engaging academics in entrepreneurship and pulling them away from teaching and research activities, which may be especially detrimental to universities if they decide to leave academia (Toole and Czarnitzki 2010), it is important to note that other forms of knowledge transfer may be more attractive/easier routes (Sandström et al. 2018), such as consultancy, licensing or collaborative/contract research. In fact, it is found that some university technology transfer offices prioritised the licensing of university intellectual property (IP) over creating academic spinout companies, as these were less risky and generated immediate cash-flow, compared with equity-tied returns associated with academic spinouts (Markman et al. 2005). However, these alternative modes of knowledge commercialisation may not generate equivalent societal outcomes, given the unique nature of academic spinouts. For example, knowledge generated through collaborative or contract research does not warrant the generation of new products or services. In the life sciences field this may mean no revolutionary cures, treatments or technologies. As such without firms such as Biontech, originally spun off from Johannes University Mainz in Germany, that pioneered mRNA vaccines against Covid-19, the world could have looked very differently now.

Overall, academic spinout companies can be defined as unique types of firms developing university-generated intellectual property that blur the boundaries between higher education and industry, pose as vehicles for knowledge translation and codification, develop non-local spatial reach manifested through their organisational growth and market access, and develop networks that are increasingly more heterophilious in character (Prokop 2023). These characteristics make academic spinout companies different not only from corporate spinouts, but also from all other types of firms. Whilst most entrepreneurs are motivated by financial returns, academic entrepreneurs tend to value a range of factors that are typically related to reputation effect and advancement of their academic careers that result from founding a company (Fini et al. 2009; Hayter 2011; Lam 2011). This is peculiar and presents difficulties for a large body of literature on the theory of the firm (Prokop 2023) to fit academic spinouts in their explanations.

CONTRIBUTION TO REGIONAL ECONOMIC DEVELOPMENT

Whilst much of the literature on academic spinout companies pays attention to how these firms are formed, their performance, or how they develop, a paucity of studies show interest in understanding the contribution of academic spinouts to local/regional economic development. This highlights a clearly under-researched and underreported area, which is paradoxical, given how much effort has been devoted to studying academic spinouts. Nonetheless, there are a number of ways in which academic spinout companies contribute to the economic development of their regions, many of them unique to spinouts.

First, the formation of academic spinout companies utilises knowledge that may not have found commercial application otherwise. This expresses the Third Mission most profoundly, as apart from economic benefits of forming a firm that creates employment, generates revenue, spends in a local or national economy and pays taxes, academic spinouts enhance the wellbeing of the society at large, through innovations expressed in products and services. Some of these products or services, especially from biotech-nology (e.g. Micropep from Centre National de la Recherche Scientifique and Toulouse University delivered a micropeptides-based biofungicide for plants) or medical device spinouts (e.g. Alesi Surgical from Cardiff University developed a visibility-improving device for laparoscopic surgery) contribute to that wellbeing directly, whilst others contribute through wider technolog-ical and economic impacts. For the extant literature, it remains difficult to quantify the socio-economic value of such innovations, as at times these may revolutionise the technological paradigms of today, very much expressing the Schumpeterian character in such a unique type of firm.

Second, academic spinout generation shows how universities can capitalise on their relationships with industry. As part of their Third Mission, univer-sities interact with firms through collaborative research, contract research, consultancy, continuing professional development courses, etc., generating income and building networks (Huggins et al. 2016), which can be accessed in the future to either engage businesses in student projects, fund further research or develop academic spinout companies. For firms engaging with universities through these multiple avenues, access to knowledge they cannot generate internally is critical to their innovation activities (Huggins, Prokop, Steffenson, Johnston and Clifton 2014). Recent evidence shows that formation of academic spinouts is explained by such heterophilious actors (Prokop and Thompson 2023) that come from outside the academia. Spinout founders employ existing industry networks in the development of their companies (D'Este et al. 2012), primarily to find out whether a particular intellectual

property has any commercial use or value, or to identify a future development pathway for it. As such, academic entrepreneurship activity channels
pre-existing university–industry networks to develop highly innovative firms
that contribute to regional economic development.

Third, academic entrepreneurship increases innovation-based entrepreneurship activity within regions, positively contributing to their competitiveness.
Whilst universities are key players in creating knowledge, not all of this
knowledge finds its way to the local/regional economy. Graduates of university
taught courses remain a key form of knowledge dissemination; however, their
knowledge is standardised, and not at the cutting edge of academic research.
This is partly related to the need for further development of their absorptive
capacity through advanced degree training. With academic entrepreneurship
such avant garde knowledge becomes transformed into new products or
services, playing a transformative role for local economies, where academic
spinout companies are based. It enables improvements in competitiveness of
such areas by increasing the stock of knowledge-based business and productivity (Huggins et al. 2021; Huggins, Izushi, Prokop and Thompson 2014).
This is especially important, as peripheral regions that struggle to generate
technology or knowledge-based firms may in return benefit from this positive
university-induced effect on local entrepreneurship and innovation activity.
For example, peripheral regions such as North East in the UK reported nearly
double the proportion of academic spinouts as of all active firms compared
with London (Prokop and Kitagawa 2022), signifying their important role in
contributing to regional competitiveness.

Fourth, studying academic spinout companies could be helpful for regional
economic development policymaking, as it reflects how regional entrepreneurial ecosystem resources and institutions are employed to support the formation
and success of these complex, knowledge-based and radically innovative firms.
Prokop and Kitagawa (2022) identified four regional archetypes by studying
the shareholder networks of UK academic spinouts. They noted that *peripheral
lock-in* type regions suffer from poor network development, reflected in lower
rates of spinout companies generated by universities in those lagging regions.
Across regions categorised as *entrepreneurial periphery* it was observed that
they have access to greater entrepreneurial opportunities, but reside in weak
networks. Such regions have some key ecosystem actors that can assist in the
entrepreneurial journey of these knowledge-based ventures, making the most
of their limited networks. Regions that follow the archetype of *rigid core* are
characterised by very strong networks which are critical in creating companies;
however, their regional ecosystems offer limited opportunities to assist with
the growth of such ventures. Regions that are classed as *entrepreneurial core*
have strongly developed networks and their ecosystems contain key actors that
offer a very good level of entrepreneurial opportunities. One thing that Prokop

and Kitagawa (2022) note, however, is that there is an institutional effect, where *peripheral lock-in* or *entrepreneurial periphery* archetypes can achieve higher success outcomes of academic spinout companies than those from *entrepreneurial core* regions, indicating an efficiency in utilising regional networks and resources. For regional economic development policymaking this effect shows that some peripheral regions may respond better to increased resources supporting their existing activities, as they may simply achieve more with them. On the other hand, the traditionally successful regions may generate sub-optimal entrepreneurial outcomes, where more resourcing effort needs to be invested to produce regional economic development (Rodríguez-Pose 2013).

Fifth, academic spinout companies are characterised by higher levels of survival than firms in the general population. This is critical, as firms that persist have a greater chance of developing their products or services, increasing their employment, and achieving long-term success that is fundamental to economic development. Typical 3- and 5-year survival rates of firms in the general population of most developed nations oscillate within 55–65% and 35–50% (Office for National Statistics (UK), US Bureau of Labour Statistics, Eurostat), respectively. For academic spinouts this is much higher. Lawton Smith et al. (2014) report 3-year survival at 92% and 5-year survival at 82% for academic spinouts from London universities. Prokop et al. (2019) report even higher rates covering most of the UK universities generating spinout companies, with 3-year survival at 95–100% and 5-year survival at 87–97%. Similar high levels were also observed in Canada at 82% after 4–5 years (Doutriaux 1987), the Netherlands (although limited to Delft University) at 90% after 6 years (Van Geenhuizen and Soetanto 2009), Italy at 86% overall (Bolzani et al. 2014), Spain at 73% (Epure et al. 2016), and the US (although again limited to a single institution – University of Michigan) at 89% (Gubitta et al. 2016). One outlier is the study by Wennberg et al. (2011) which reports that Swedish spinouts reported lower survival rates at 73% after 2 years and 53% after 5 years, which are still considerably positive outcomes, for one of the few university intellectual property regimes where IP is owned by academics and not the university. Such high levels of survival are critical to regional economic development, which in addition to employment and tax revenue enables organisational learning and business leadership development that may have wider effects on other firms within the locale.

Sixth, the economic impact of academic spinout companies greatly exceeds the public spending devoted to academic research. In his study on the impact of Canadian spinouts, Vincett (2010) observed that government expenditure on academic research generates economic returns of between four to six times the value of that investment, in addition to further long-term positive impacts of companies surviving beyond the studied period of time. As such, academic spinout companies not only offer a strong argument for support of university Third Mission activities, but also synergistically present policymakers with very convincing arguments to continue and potentially increase investment in university research. These high rates of economic returns also offer long-term economic solutions to peripheral regions, where universities could play key economic roles in transforming their areas. Whilst there are arguments against placing such a heavy burden on universities, where this may thwart alternative economic development strategies (Brown 2016), universities clearly show the ability to exercise a significant impact on their regions. In fact, universities that have observed cuts to public funding of academic research may rely on technology commercialisation activities, in particular, those related to higher returns such as academic spinouts, to improve their institutional budgets (Clarysse et al. 2007; Grimaldi et al. 2011).

Seventh, successful academic spinouts contribute to innovation activity and innovativeness of industry, positively contributing to economic development. In a study by Bonardo et al. (2011) it was found that spinout companies raising capital on stock exchanges tend to invest more intensively in research and development activity than other listed firms. This is particularly important, as increasing innovation activity, being a key driver of regional economic development, is a critical goal for policymakers to stimulate growth (Howells 2005). Nevertheless, there are not many academic spinouts that make it to the stock exchange, and in fact, there is a higher proportion of them securing further success through acquisitions (Lawton Smith et al. 2008), where these are particularly regarded as more desirable by academic spinouts (Nerkar and Shane 2003), allowing venture capitalists to exit their investments. Such acquired spinout companies represent a major technology transfer to larger established firms that may lack the innovation capabilities or absorptive capacity to utilise knowledge otherwise available. As such, academic spinout companies contribute to regional economic development by either directly stimulating innovation activity or enhancing the innovation capability of existing stock of firms.

Eighth, academic spinout companies are conduits for knowledge spillover within regions. Whilst universities generate a great deal of new knowledge, its accessibility may prove difficult through direct interactions of businesses with universities. Some of the key challenges in such interactions are related to university bureaucracy and contractual issues (Huggins, Prokop, Steffenson, Johnston and Clifton 2014), highlighting the increased transaction costs of sourcing knowledge from universities. Contrastingly, academic spinout companies act as intermediaries (Prokop 2023) between the two environments of academia and industry, frequently overcoming transaction costs in access to skilled researchers (Huggins, Prokop, Steffenson, Johnston and Clifton 2014) or in collaboration with universities, where spinout companies extend commercial research activities of university departments (Prokop 2021). This distinctive role suggests that for peripheral regions in particular, academic spinouts can lead to the development of connections between universities and the regional business community (Benneworth and Charles 2005). They become conduits for knowledge spillover, where academics learn about commercial interactions through spinout companies, enabling them to engage more widely with firms in the region. In fact, such knowledge, if frequently accessed by the business community, could be considered a territorial knowledge pool (Benneworth and Charles 2005), improving regional innovation performance by contributing to the activities of other firms in the region (Bagchi-Sen et al. 2022).

Ninth, academic spinouts play a key role in formation of clusters. Whilst cluster formation is not solely dependent on academic spinout companies, they have played an important role in the growth of Silicon Valley (Saxenian 1994), where companies started up at Stanford University helped develop a critical mass of technology entrepreneurship in the area. Similarly, in Cambridge (UK) academic spinout companies played a critical role in the development of the cluster (Garnsey and Heffernan 2005). Principally, they added to the stock of technology-based firms creating demand for specialist labour with advanced degrees. What is important in this entrepreneurship volume development is that academic spinout companies tend to locate close to universities they spun-off from (Di Gregorio and Shane 2003; Bagchi-Sen et al. 2022), making them a potent transformative entrepreneurial power for regional economies. Academic spinouts have also participated in the development of local social capital that was critical to transforming Cambridge into a cluster (Garnsey and Heffernan 2005). This network building was not only based on forming linkages between firms and the university in the area, but it was also reliant on further (corporate) spin-off activity, where employees from the incumbent firms would create new firms to develop technologies that their original employers would not. By contributing to cluster development, spinout companies have a critical role to play in transforming regions hosting universities, increasing the level of sectoral specialisation of their respective economies and boosting productivity.

Tenth, a very important contribution of academic spinout companies is the creation of high-quality and value-added jobs in the region. Academic spinouts are found to generate higher employment growth than other knowledge-based firms (Barbosa and Faria 2020), indicating a performance premium, where they outperform non-spinout firms as a consequence of having the 'unfavourable' academic origins (Czarnitzki et al. 2014). Furthermore, they create jobs for graduates with advanced degrees (Shane 2004), given their higher requirements for the levels of absorptive capacity needed to translate cutting-edge academic research. This high-skilled employment is related to the greater efficiency of academic spinout companies (Epure et al. 2016). Given that most of the academic spinouts tend to stay local to their parent universities (Shane 2004; Bagchi-Sen et al. 2022), much of the employment they create is also in the parent university's region, signifying a critical role in localised economic development impacts. Such proximity is also beneficial to the academic spinout company itself since being close to the parent university provides it with better access to highly skilled graduates and academic staff (e.g. talented postdoctoral researchers) for employment or research collaboration (Shane 2004).

Whilst there are clearly many positive contributions of academic spinout companies to regional economic development, critique directed at spinouts suggests that the picture is more complex. In their paper studying regional development impacts of spinout companies from Queen's University, Belfast, Harrison and Leitch (2010) point out that their contribution is overstated since many of these companies remain small and have limited potential for growth. As such, it is difficult to attribute the transformative regional economic development expectations to academic spinouts. Furthermore, generating academic spinout companies may lead to an academic 'brain drain' effect (Toole and Czarnitzki 2010). Academic entrepreneurs who also remain in their university positions were observed to generate fewer publications and patents (Toole and Czarnitzki 2010), limiting their productivity at universities. In fact, this effect is even worse when they decide to leave academia in order to focus on academic spinout companies, completely stopping their academic productivity. This may limit the ability of regional economies to employ talent efficiently, where their work could have wider and longer-term economic effects when producing knowledge, compared with exploiting a single piece of intellectual property (Toole and Czarnitzki 2010).

Furthermore, there are instances where academics are sued by their universities or technology transfer offices for privately patenting intellectual property (Grimaldi et al. 2011), leading to unnecessary conflict and knowledge productivity loss, and discouraging academic entrepreneurship activity. Additionally, policymakers' attention attracted to academic spinout companies may result in policy strategies that incentivise creating knowledge that has more immediate commercial potential, as this is more likely to lead to academic spinout formation (Abreu and Grinevich 2013), rather than basic knowledge for which it takes more time to identify its applicability. This may lead to an increase in short-term economic goals at the cost of long-term development, potentially discouraging academic talent from such regional or national policy regimes.

Finally, universities that wish to benefit from academic entrepreneurship activity may decide to devote significant efforts to develop university entrepreneurial ecosystems (Prokop 2021), without realising that many cannot generate enough research to feed the ecosystem with spinout ventures, leading to inefficient use of university resources. The underlying basic ingredient for academic spinout formation remains the production of knowledge and resultant disclosures (Lockett and Wright 2005; Prokop and Thompson 2023), without which no technology transfer may take place. This is partly why much of the academic entrepreneurship activity has been observed at top universities that generate a significant volume of knowledge (e.g. Bagchi-Sen et al. 2022; Lawton Smith et al. 2008; Shane 2004).

THE UNIVERSITY ENTREPRENEURIAL ECOSYSTEM

Regional economic development impact is an outcome of the performance of university entrepreneurial ecosystems (UEEs). Much like broader entrepreneurial ecosystems (EEs), university entrepreneurial ecosystems generate Schumpeterian entrepreneurship (Mason and Brown 2014), with radical innovations, the utilisation of high-quality human capital and high-growth potential (Bonardo et al. 2011; Czarnitzki et al. 2014; Ortín-Ángel and Vendrell-Herrero 2014). The academic entrepreneur and academic spinout – the venture – are at the centre of university entrepreneurial ecosystems. However, unlike typical place-based ecosystems, universities play critical roles in university entrepreneurial ecosystems.

Given the above discussions, university roles are characterised as follows: (a) they *generate talent* that feeds the ecosystem's actors and influences their performance and the variety of actors; (b) they *share* locally produced *knowledge* that is partly processed by academic spinouts in their enzymatic role or realised fully by academic spinouts; (c) they *exercise transformative power* over their regions by the generation of knowledge, talent and entrepreneurship; (d) as anchor tenants they reveal their *organisational capability* in structuring the ecosystem's composition (Prokop 2022) and employing regional networks of ecosystem actors; (e) as clear *leaders* they define the trajectory of performance and the knowledge-base of the university entrepreneurial ecosystems; (f) they *generate entrepreneurship* in multiple forms and at a variety of innovation levels – academic spinouts, staff startups, and graduate startups (Kitagawa et al. 2022); (g) (but) they only have a degree of *control over generating entrepreneurship* in the form of academic spinout companies that show superior survival characteristics to other types of firms; and (h) *to produce entrepreneurship* in the form of academic spinout companies universities build and *employ* local and regional *networks*, showing their connectedness, embeddedness and cooperative nature.

These roles define university entrepreneurial ecosystems and highlight their unique character that separates them from the extant theorising of broader or generic entrepreneurial ecosystems (e.g. Spigel 2017; Stam 2015; Stam and Van de Ven 2021), which do not identify central ecosystem actors (except for entrepreneurs) and where universities are just part of a set of ecosystem elements rather than the core element. Consequently, university entrepreneurial ecosystems set up predominantly to generate academic spinout companies reveal ecosystems that are configured for cutting-edge technology firms that the generic entrepreneurial ecosystems literature deems critical, but struggles to articulate theories that produce such specific outputs.

This set of distinctive features of university entrepreneurial ecosystems pre-conditions them to generate outcomes that may surpass the economic development level of their respective regions (Prokop and Kitagawa 2022), making them crucial development architectures. In fact, in university entrepreneurial ecosystems, the universities act as ecosystem engines that power them, or in poorly performing ones, starve them of this vital energy supply.

University entrepreneurial ecosystems are composed of many actors that perform similar roles to generic entrepreneurial ecosystems (Prokop and Thompson 2023), but principally include the following (Prokop 2021, 2023): universities, technology transfer offices, academic spinout companies, business incubators and science parks, investors – in multiple forms that include business angels and venture capitalists, academic founders/entrepreneurs and external management talent, often referred to as external entrepreneurs (Franklin et al. 2001). In addition to these, university entrepreneurial eco-systems include further elements such as: entrepreneur support programs, national programmes and policies, culture and locational factors (Hayter et al. 2018), many of which when studied individually or as part of university entrepreneurial ecosystems have been found to be important to academic spinout activity (Prokop et al. 2019; Shane 2004). In the development of this emergent literature on university entrepreneurial ecosystems it was found that the composition of these elements – or their presence in the university entre-preneurial ecosystems – is related to higher levels of generation of academic spinout companies (Prokop 2022). At the same time, even when these elements are present, their configuration may lead to diverse outputs (Prokop 2021), indicating a very complex nature of university entrepreneurial ecosystems.

CONCLUSION

The academic spinout company is a unique type of firm that intermediates between two typically disconnected worlds: university and private industry. As a consequence of this original character, spinout companies have a wide-ranging ability to contribute to regional economic development that includes even potentially transformative effects on the innovation capability of local firms, regional competitiveness and cluster creation. This 'gluing' role shows how academic spinout companies are critical to developing and densi-fying regional networks that connect actors into a university entrepreneurial ecosystem.

Whilst university entrepreneurial ecosystems may function and perform differently, their existence plays a vital role in development of areas hosting universities. Crucially, universities are ecosystem engines that power these architectures, input knowledge, generate talent, build and organise networks, lead their development and produce entrepreneurship. Although universities generate multiple types of entrepreneurship, the remaining parts of the book focus on the type that is most critical to university entrepreneurial ecosystems and regional economic development literatures by embodying all of the unique characteristics discussed above, namely academic spinout companies.

3.   Spinouts and commercialisation: ecosystems not just an urban phenomenon

Whilst much of the broad entrepreneurial ecosystems literature is dominated by empirical studies of urban areas, university entrepreneurial ecosystems may exist outside of the urban sphere, in predominantly rural areas. Following the presence of university entrepreneurial ecosystems in England, the chapter aims to show that rural localities may host university entrepreneurial ecosystems. Further to that, the chapter examines differences between the urban and rural characteristics of university entrepreneurial ecosystems to finally reflect on the challenges of such spatial character.

CREATING A SPINOUT COMPANY

Entrepreneurial intentions of academics are clearly important to academic spinout company formation. However, given that there has been a shift to normalise knowledge commercialisation activities as part of a portfolio of academic duties (Compagnucci and Spigarelli 2020), other factors may play important roles in spinout activity. These can be considered under three types representing different dimensions of university entrepreneurial ecosystems: (a) university factors; (b) spatial factors; and (c) network factors.

University Factors

The university as a key actor of the university entrepreneurial ecosystem has a capability to critically influence academic entrepreneurship output. As the essential ingredient for a recipe to create academic spinout companies is knowledge, universities characterised by attracting greater research funding tend to form more spinout companies (Lockett and Wright 2005). This is found to be particularly important when such funding is linked to industry sources (Di Gregorio and Shane 2003; O'Shea et al. 2005), as links with industry enable opportunity identification (D'Este et al. 2012), given that academics may not be the most knowledgeable about market needs. Furthermore, the intellectual eminence of the university – related to rankings and institution's prestige – is also positively associated with academic spinout formation (Di Gregorio and Shane 2003; Lawton Smith et al. 2008). This is partly because institutions that have international reputation for excellence typically attract academic talent – the so-called 'star scientists', who have a greater propensity to create spinout ventures (Toole and Czarnitzki 2007; Gilsing et al. 2010), but also are more likely to attract the income that funds research underpinning spinout formation (Vohora et al. 2004; Lawton Smith et al. 2008).

Generating knowledge is critical, but so are institutional policies that encourage and support academic entrepreneurship (Lockett et al. 2003). Without these, many academics may dismiss the idea of doing something that their employers would be against – in the 'ivory towers' that have been characterised by resistance to Third Mission activity (Haeussler and Colyvas 2011). Universities that developed policies to support academic spinout generation, such as leave of absence or support in resolving intellectual property disputes, had greater numbers of spinout companies (Shane 2004). Other policies that universities may implement are related to allowing academic staff taking equity stakes in spinout companies (Di Gregorio and Shane 2003) or specifying royalty share (Bekkers et al. 2006), promoting entrepreneurial activity, offering incubation services for new ventures or supporting spinouts with preferential access to expensive university laboratories and equipment (Fini et al. 2011). It is important to note that university policies tend to be designed for achieving particular goals; when these policies are tuned to increase the formation of spinout companies alone, their quality may suffer (Fini et al. 2017), as is the case with the broader configuration of university entrepreneurial ecosystems (Prokop 2021).

One of such policies used to be manifested through formation of technology transfer offices, now quite widespread across universities, either internal university departments or externalised units registered as private companies owned by universities (e.g. Wisconsin Alumni Research Foundation from University of Wisconsin; Imperial Innovations from Imperial College London). Technology transfer offices run privately enable universities to overcome internal policy limitations to deliver on their commercialisation goals (Jain and George 2007). Lack of this autonomy may subject the Technology Transfer Offices (TTOs) run as internal university departments to organisational politics, for example – to patent inventions that have no commercial potential, but ensure the retention of star scientists (Kenney and Patton 2009). At the same time, the private character of TTOs may force them to be profit-oriented at the cost of commercialising technologies that either require more development or where commercial opportunities are more difficult to identify. This is especially important as it may limit the full potential of the Third Mission of universities, especially when the cutting-edge knowledge they generate may be decades away from the technological paradigm that markets operate in.

Whilst academic spinout companies are an important focus of TTO activities, their breadth of functions is much greater, as TTOs typically oversee all university–industry interactions, deal with patenting and licensing, identify disclosures, develop networks with venture capitalists and other local or regional investors, and in addition form connections with external management talent to recruit into spinout companies to assist academic founders with building the companies (Holgersson and Aaboen 2019; Good et al. 2019; BVCA/Library House 2005). A well-resourced and supportive TTO, with experienced professionals, may generate more academic spinout companies (Siegel et al. 2004; Fini et al. 2011). It is important to note that the decision whether to form a spinout company or follow an alternative commercialisation route rests with technology transfer offices, and their different priorities may influence entrepreneurial activity (Markman et al. 2005). Nonetheless, such decisions can only be made if the university generates a sufficient level of research, without which developing technology transfer office capabilities is strategically ineffective in delivering spinout companies (Hewitt-Dundas 2012).

Having resources and institutional-level policies is not the only important set of factors in the formation of spinout companies. In fact, many studies point out that the organisational culture of the university or at a departmental level is vital to encouraging entrepreneurial activity (Shane 2004; Brooksbank and Thomas 2001). This is especially pronounced in university departments where the chair is engaged in disclosing inventions (Bercovitz and Feldman 2008), showing positive role models but also normalising commercialisation activity. From a broader perspective, it is important to observe that universities' approach to commercialisation of inventions is also influenced by local culture (Braunerhjelm 2007), which may also partly explain why this activity is more entrenched in the US or UK compared with European or Asian universities (Lehrer and Asakawa 2004). As such, there are clearly spatial implications for academic spinout company formation, reflected in the characteristics of the locale.

Spatial Factors

Whilst the formation of academic spinout companies is critically dependent on universities, the local or regional environment of the university may also be important. In their study of Italian spinout generation Fini et al. (2011) highlight that the entrepreneurial ecosystem plays a vital role, especially expressed through regional networks and the availability of finance in the university region. This suggests that places with greater stocks of social capital, typically more densely populated urban areas, offer more fertile ground for development of academic spinout companies. This is partly confirmed in a study by Prokop

(2021) where urban-based universities tended to form stronger university entrepreneurial ecosystems predominantly because they had greater access to local or regional networks that supported spinout formation.

Additionally, the wider macro socio-economic environment should not be discounted in its association with academic spinout formation, in particular related to lower regional levels of research and development spending, population or employment rate (Fini et al. 2017). Such findings suggest that the formation of academic spinout companies may thrive in smaller peripheral regions that underperform economically and show lower innovation levels. This may reflect the transformative regional role of university entrepreneurial ecosystems that show more efficiency in stimulating entrepreneurial activity in less developed regional environments (Prokop and Kitagawa 2022). However, it is also important to observe that at a wider national level the differences in academic spinout generation may be linked to intellectual property rights policies (Fini et al. 2017), revealing that these spatial differences are multi-scalar in character.

Whilst many case studies of university spinout formation have focused on urban-based university entrepreneurial ecosystems (e.g. Harmon et al. 1997; Benneworth and Charles 2005; Lawton Smith et al. 2014), there is a limited understanding of the non-urban university entrepreneurial ecosystems. This is perhaps the outcome of the typical best-university or best-case or best-practice approaches that are often employed in academic research yet, although informative, offer a very skewed picture of the phenomena they try to understand, often leading policymakers to wrong conclusions. Importantly, each university entrepreneurial ecosystem, location or region it occupies is unique and based on a set of distinctive socio-economic conditions, which cannot be transplanted between areas. This idiosyncratic character has been depicted in Prokop (2021), where four extreme cases of university entrepreneurial ecosystems showed a myriad of spatial configurations leading to a diversity of outputs. For example, it is not possible to move a concentration of management team talent from a knowledge-based cluster such as London to the Highlands in Scotland, or from Silicon Valley to Billings in Montana, and any policy grounded in misreading such aspects would fail to generate the desired outcomes. This chapter tries to bring attention to this issue, as well as highlight the importance of considering the spatial character of university entrepreneurial ecosystems.

Network Factors

The importance of relational space is strongly acknowledged in the academic entrepreneurship literature (Huggins et al. 2020; Sousa-Ginel et al. 2017; Aaboen et al. 2016), yet limited studies link the character of networks to spinout formation. This is a critical element that in university entrepreneurial ecosystems leads to greater numbers of academic spinout companies. In particular, university entrepreneurial ecosystem actors that have a heterophilious character – not associated with or controlled by university – are positively related to forming spinout companies, for example, expressed through connections to other university entrepreneurial ecosystems (Prokop and Thompson 2023).

Interestingly, the presence of heterophilious actors is more likely in areas of greater population and concentration of firms, typically seen in urban areas, where small rural places would tend to reach network closure owing to limited numbers of actors and actor types. University entrepreneurial ecosystems in such locations may reach out to other more urban areas to limit the lock-in effects of local homophily (Prokop 2021). Additionally, university entrepreneurial ecosystems with their anchor tenant more engaged and centrally positioned in networks with industry are related to greater academic spinout formation activity (Huggins et al. 2020), indicating the importance of network structure of university entrepreneurial ecosystems and the university's ability to occupy a central position within them.

WHAT HAPPENS TO A SPINOUT COMPANY POST-FORMATION?

The development of academic spinouts is very distinctive. It takes a multi-stage route that begins with academic research (Vohora et al. 2004), followed by opportunity recognition, where disclosure may be registered, development of the proof of concept to test whether the underlying intellectual property is workable, and finally the founding of a company (Degroof and Roberts 2004; Clarysse et al. 2005; Rasmussen 2011). An avid observer may notice that three of these stages are clearly before the academic spinout even takes a legal form of a company. It is often also at this pre-formation phase that technology transfer officers will try to recruit an external and experienced management team and engage with investors, either business angels or venture capitalists (Prokop 2021), tapping into the resources of their university entrepreneurial ecosystems.

Whilst this is not a common practice among all university entrepreneurial ecosystems, depending on individual configurations, some university entrepreneurial ecosystems let specialised venture capitalists select a disclosure and develop it from this pre-formation stage (Prokop 2017). In other cases, technology transfer offices will consider such academic spinout projects to remain in the pre-formation stage until at least the management team can be formed. Interestingly, whilst technology transfer officers are so focused on portraying a credible company by building the management team, venture capitalists investing in spinouts are not (BVCA/Library House 2005). The two most important aspects venture capitalists seek out in academic spinouts are the technology's market potential and likelihood of exit (BVCA/Library House 2005), clearly suggesting that university entrepreneurial ecosystems may suffer from a lack of coherent goals and expectations across their key actors. This incoherence could potentially manifest itself more visibly in university entrepreneurial ecosystems that are less developed, perhaps in an emergent phase, compared with those that show strong performance (Colombelli et al. 2019; Roundy et al. 2018; Prokop 2021).

Once the academic spinout company is born, it often requires a registered office. Although academic entrepreneurship literature expected spinouts to transition to business incubators, science parks or accelerators (Shane 2004), the reality is that most of them remain in university departments, which act as incubation spaces (Hewitt-Dundas 2015). There is a very good reason for this, as academic spinouts require close access to advanced lab equipment in order to further develop their technology. Given the fact that universities take substantial equity stakes in academic spinouts, this departmental incubation is very pragmatic to universities. On one hand this arrangement limits the operating costs of academic spinout companies, which is critical when initial seed or venture capital investments are either small or non-existent. On the other hand, this incubation benefits the academic spinout by tapping into proximity benefits for academic founders, who can work on the technology in their spare time, in the labs they are familiar with, without a need to travel to another set of premises.

Whilst much of the literature depicts post-formation development as typically the last stage (e.g. Ndonzuau et al. 2002; Parmentola and Ferretti 2018), this is perhaps when further distinct stages of growth will take place. An alternative model of academic spinout development follows their post-formation evolution of shareholder networks (Prokop and Kitagawa 2022), finding that after the company is founded it enters an organisation phase where the spinout's shareholder networks grow intensively until the company reaches the age of 6–9 years. Such shareholder development may provide necessary network access to resources that stimulate firm growth. In the subsequent 7–10 years they observe an exploitation phase, where the growth of shareholder networks stabilises. From the age of 19 onwards, the academic spinouts enter the maturing and reorganisation phase where their networks are continuously reshaped to prevent homophilious lock-in, which may undermine their survival (Prokop et al. 2019). This is especially difficult, as team building in companies tends to follow homophily, even when the extant knowledge suggests this may be negatively related to firm's performance (Parker 2009). In this post-formation development depiction academic spinouts clearly portray a high level of network dynamism that cannot be depicted with a single stage.

Overall, these multiple development stages build a complex picture of academic spinout companies, with at least half of the stages recognising pre-formation development activities. Given that academic spinouts tend to stay in spatial proximity to their parent universities, this network dynamism is critical for the local economy university entrepreneurial ecosystems occupy.

SPINOUT COMPANIES OUTSIDE THE URBAN AREAS

To respond to the limited interest in non-urban university entrepreneurial ecosystems, I aim to show that rural localities should not be dismissed and unacknowledged in studying university entrepreneurial ecosystems. In fact, this spatial character should stimulate creative policy-intended reflections on solutions to assist a wider spectrum of university entrepreneurial ecosystems, recognising the wider local environment they are embedded within. Some of these university entrepreneurial ecosystems are well known, but the rural nature of their surroundings is rarely acknowledged or considered in the literature.

Data

The data used to investigate the academic spinout activity of rural university entrepreneurial ecosystems focuses geographically on the English universities. Whilst most of England's universities are based in urban locations, a modest number of them are in rural regions, where the university town or city is the only urban area (Charles 2016; Salomaa et al. 2022). To classify regions where university entrepreneurial ecosystems reside I use the urban rural classification of DEFRA (Department for Environment, Food & Rural Affairs) at the county and unitary authority area level. DEFRA provides online tables (DEFRA 2021) that list all areas based on 2011 Local Authority Rural Urban Classification. Rural areas are considered here those that DEFRA classes as 'Largely Rural' or 'Mainly Rural' – jointly signifying that 50% or more of the population of such locations reside in rural areas, whilst I denote the urban character of areas reflecting the following set of classifications: 'Urban with Significant Rural', 'Urban with Minor Conurbation', 'Urban with Major Conurbation' and 'Urban with City and Town', all with less than 50% of their populations residing in rural areas.

For university entrepreneurial ecosystem data I use the UK's HEBCIS (Higher Education Business and Community Interaction survey), which has been collecting metrics related to Third Mission activity for the past two decades. The aggregate data presented below focus on 60 English universities (approximately half of higher education institutions in England), excluding arts and specialist colleges (or institutes). Universities that did not respond to HEBCIS, recorded no activity in terms of disclosures over the past 7 years or hold no stock of active spinouts are also removed. This does not mean that the excluded universities are disengaged from Third Mission activities or do not generate disclosures (some even generated spinouts, but recorded no disclosures, or disclosures but not spinouts); in fact, many of these universities take other routes to create impact in their regional communities, for example through public lectures, continuous professional development or consultancy. Consequently, the dataset captures eight universities based in rural areas. The majority of these universities are research oriented, with two top English institutions captured: the University of Cambridge and the University of Oxford.

Results

Overall, rural universities show some remarkable performance in terms of academic entrepreneurship (Table 3.1), partly owing to the effects of Cambridge and Oxford universities. However, when this effect is excluded the remaining six rural universities perform on average just slightly below the urban institutions, showing their remarkable strength in knowledge commercialisation activity. The rural university entrepreneurial ecosystems on average show higher level of completeness than urban ones. When examining the individual completeness data, Oxford Brookes is the only underdeveloped university entrepreneurial ecosystem, which can be explained by its more teaching-oriented activity, observed through lower levels of disclosures or stock of patents. Its university entrepreneurial ecosystem includes only two elements: entrepreneurship training and business advice, but misses on important incubation and finance components. In comparison, Cranfield UEE holds a slightly higher stock of patents, but generates higher levels of disclosures and its university entrepreneurial ecosystem is complete, as reflected in the performance of its spinouts (survival, employment).

University entrepreneurial ecosystems positioned within wider rural localities tend to be built around research-intensive universities. Their average stocks of spinouts compare favourably with those of university entrepreneurial ecosystems from urban areas. Not all spinouts generated by university entrepreneurial ecosystems reach the development level when they could be sold. However, on average the rural universities generate higher incomes from academic spinout equity sales than their urban counterparts. When observing Prokop's (2021) filtration levels, depicting the ratio of spinouts generated from disclosures, it is notable that most of the rural university entrepreneurial ecosystems run rather tight filtration models, with only Cranfield UEE showing a looser one.

What this shows is that even university entrepreneurial ecosystems that do not generate many disclosures and spinouts, but are characterised by high

Table 3.1   Academic entrepreneurship activity of rural university entrepreneurial ecosystems in England

Rural university entrepreneurial ecosystems	Stock of active spinouts in 2020/21	FTE employment of active spinouts in 2020/21	Sale of equity in spinouts between 2014/15 & 2020/21 [£000]	Share of IP income from sale of equity in spinouts between 2014/15 & 2020/21	Disclosures between 2014/15 & 2020/21	Stock of patents in 2020/21	Prokop's (2021) filtration between 2014/15 & 2020/21	Survival rates 1959–2014* (%)	University entrepreneurial ecosystem completeness, 2015/16** (%)
Cambridge	130	1,978	49,056	0.398	1,612	1,212	0.036	85.00	100.00
Cranfield	8	83	0	0.000	156	48	0.083	100.00	100.00
Durham	22	402	5,961	0.927	335	204	0.036	60.87	85.71
East Anglia	10	145	1,018	0.102	373	192	0.016	100.00	100.00
Exeter	16	68	1,592	0.659	300	105	0.027	75.00	85.71
Hull	1	16	0	0.000	105	73	0.000	100.00	85.71
Oxford Brookes	1	16	0	0.000	23	33	0.043	100.00	28.57
Oxford	168	5,632	43,410	0.136	2,526	4,455	0.047	83.50	100.00
Rural***	44.50	1,042.50	12,629.63	0.204	678.75	790.25	0.066	88.05	85.71
Urban***	14.12	164.94	3,016.23	0.320	321.67	243.71	0.044	74.63	82.61
All***	18.17	281.95	4,298.02	0.262	369.28	316.58	0.049	76.55	83.10

Notes: FTE, Full-time equivalent. Prokop's (2021) filtration level = spinout companies/number of disclosures. The data include eight rural universities and 52 urban-based ones.

Source: * Prokop (2017), however the data represent only 48 of the 52 urban universities presented here; ** HEBCIS, building on Prokop's (2022) composition; the UEE completeness includes the following seven elements – on-campus incubator, off-campus incubator, science park, entrepreneurship training, seed corn investment, venture capital and business advice; *** average.

levels of ecosystem completeness, choose to be very careful and selective in their formation of academic spinout companies, in some instances, like Hull UEE, perhaps not employing their ecosystems effectively. This could be a result of such university entrepreneurial ecosystems not configured for spinout formation (Prokop 2021), given the higher levels of survival achieved among the rural university entrepreneurial ecosystems. It is also crucial to observe that ecosystem actors that remain under-utilised may become obsolete, potentially leading to a decline (but not death) of the university entrepreneurial ecosystem (Mack and Mayer 2016). In such cases the university entrepreneurial ecosystems may undergo a restructuring or reconfiguration to adapt to a new equilibrium (Roundy et al. 2018; Scott et al. 2021). This may be characterised by changes in composition of the university entrepreneurial ecosystems, where entrepreneurial activities would shift potentially from academic spinouts to graduate startups and where disclosure numbers would drop, as these would be no longer filtered by the ecosystem (Prokop 2021).

THE CHALLENGES OF RURAL ECOSYSTEMS

Highly Diverse Ecosystems

Whilst overall there is a very positive picture of rural university entrepreneurial ecosystems, the strong influence of Cambridge and Oxford UEEs cannot be discounted. These two university entrepreneurial ecosystems clearly outperform all other university entrepreneurial ecosystems in Table 3.1. This can be largely attributed to their historical evolution into well-performing ecosystems, but also a result that is linked to a presence of very successful clusters operating in these locations strongly connected with the leading universities (Garnsey and Heffernan 2005; Huggins 2008; Waters and Lawton Smith 2008). As such, the picture of rural university entrepreneurial ecosystems shows a larger variation, with some university entrepreneurial ecosystems having low stocks of academic spinout companies (e.g. Hull, East Anglia, Cranfield).

At the same time, these contrasts cannot be better exemplified than by the two university entrepreneurial ecosystems based in Oxford. The extant literature on generic entrepreneurial ecosystems not recognising sub-ecosystems would suggest that these should be part of a single ecosystem; they should access similar ecosystem elements. Yet what is observable is that Oxford Brookes UEE and Oxford UEE, both occupying the same geographical space, show clear sub-system characteristics, with the former having a very low level of university entrepreneurial ecosystem completeness compared with the latter. The dominance of Oxford UEE is not new (e.g. Lawton Smith and Ho 2006); however, given the passage of time, Oxford Brookes UEE does not reveal characteristics of a sub-ecosystem that would increase its connectedness with the wider place-based ecosystem, indicating an interesting problem for students of entrepreneurial ecosystem evolution. On one hand, the evolutionary processes related to increasing coherence and place-based network dynamics should suggest stronger integration of disparate but co-located sub-ecosystems. On the other hand, evidence of this is difficult to identify here. This suggests that the continuing underlying feature of all entrepreneurial ecosystems is the reliance on knowledge generated within and its filtration or transformation into entrepreneurial activities (discussed in more detail in Chapter 6).

Disconnect and Discounted Performance

Given the fact that nearly all these rural university entrepreneurial ecosystems are anchored around a research-intensive institution, except for Cambridge and Oxford UEEs, they show lower levels of stock of patents and generation of disclosures than their urban counterparts. The rural character appears to exert a scientific discount on the research and commercialisation performance of rural university entrepreneurial ecosystems.

   An explanation for this could be sought in the limited access to other urban areas and relatedly more limited presence of firms and clusters leading to the under-utilisation or underperformance of such university entrepreneurial ecosystems. Rural firms have a lower propensity to engage with universities than urban-based firms (Johnston and Prokop 2021), leaving many rural-based university entrepreneurial ecosystems quite disconnected or incoherent in terms of their development (Colombelli et al. 2019; Roundy et al. 2018). One of the reasons behind this could be the mismatch between what the local firms need and what their university, a core ecosystem actor, is able to deliver (Charles 2016). At the same time, it is likely that rural university entrepreneurial ecosystems serve their surroundings through other Third Mission routes than academic spinout company formation, for example consultancy or continuing professional development, potentially placing a stronger economic development burden on them (Brown 2016).

Miscalibrated Filtration Penalty

Having high levels of university entrepreneurial ecosystem completeness does not translate well into academic spinout numbers for many of the rural university entrepreneurial ecosystems (for example, Exeter UEE or East Anglia UEE), suggesting that their filtration models are wrongly calibrated (Prokop 2021). This may be a result of disclosure identification process being inefficient or ineffective, or institutional inability in recognising commercial potential of knowledge generated at university by the ecosystem, or that the knowledge produced is of limited commercial potential, either having no applied nature, or owing to it being too advanced for the current technological paradigm of the markets.

A similar situation can be observed with the outcome of late-stage filtration (Prokop 2021), where incomes from sales of equity in academic spinout companies are low (for example Cranfield UEE). Such equity sales are generally rare events, since these take a longer time frame to materialise (Markman et al. 2005). However, they indicate that the stock of spinouts is too young for exits or the the ecosystem does not deliver exits, i.e. venture capital investments are not driving growth in value of the companies, all leading to a similar conclusion, suggesting that the filtration models of such ecosystems are not performance-oriented. Consequently, the rural character of these university entrepreneurial ecosystems induces a calibration penalty, where greater contact with industry acts as a tuning mechanism for entrepreneurial activity (Bienkowska and Klofsten 2012; Prokop and Thompson 2023), whilst its lack places filtration models in a persisting state of disequilibrium.

Network Lock-in

Rural university entrepreneurial ecosystems may offer benefits related to living conditions, peaceful villages around university towns/cities with greener areas, that may attract high-quality human capital. As such the ruralness may force a higher concentration of human capital in the core university town or city, where most employers would be based, promoting coherence development (Garnsey and Heffernan 2005). However, network homophily is more likely to develop in such contexts than in wider urban areas, as rural university entrepreneurial ecosystems may offer very unique features to attract human capital that may not have a wider appeal of urban areas.

Whilst Cambridge and Oxford show the ability to attract external talent and avoid homophilious lock-in (Sharafizad and Brown 2020), other rural institutions do not appear to be in the same position; given their performance across measures presented in Table 3.1, lock-in is a possible explanation. Network lock-in leads to limited flow of new ideas, imposes performance penalties through group-think (Barnes et al. 2004) and may lead to a decline of a university entrepreneurial ecosystem (Crespo et al. 2014).

CONCLUSION

Formation of academic spinout companies and their later growth have a clear spatial character, where university entrepreneurial ecosystems play critical roles by leaning on their local actors and benefiting from their self-organisation.

However, it is important to note that each university entrepreneurial ecosystem is based in different spatial settings, and even those that are co-located build independent ecosystems that may show different levels of connections to available local actors. This is particularly unique for rural university entrepreneurial ecosystems that find themselves in potentially disadvantaged contexts, where it may be harder to achieve good levels of performance. Nonetheless, given the successful examples of Cambridge and Oxford UEEs, there is a potential for rural university entrepreneurial ecosystems to overcome their challenges.

4. Actors of university entrepreneurial ecosystems

This chapter devotes attention to actors of university entrepreneurial ecosystems, explaining their roles and how these change over time. These include universities, technology transfer offices, spinout companies, incubation facilities, faculty, students, management talent, and investors. The chapter also makes a distinction between an academic spinout company-focused university entrepreneurial ecosystem and a campus entrepreneurial ecosystem that devotes attention towards student or graduate startups. To account for the temporality of outcomes and actor roles it proposes an evolving model of university entrepreneurial ecosystem. The framework employs an academic spinout perspective on how the actors and their importance change as the company goes through its development phases.

THE COMPOSITION OF UNIVERSITY ENTREPRENEURIAL ECOSYSTEMS

Just like broader entrepreneurial ecosystems, university ones are composed of a set of elements represented by actors who form the ecosystem, exercise control over particular ecosystem processes, and play roles that evolve over time. A good starting point to consider the actor types is Stam's (2015) framework which depicts 10 elements: networks, leadership, finance, talent, knowledge, support services, formal institutions, culture, physical infrastructure, and demand. Spigel's (2017) model of an entrepreneurial ecosystem accounts for worker talent, investment, mentors and role models, universities, support services, physical infrastructure, open markets, policy and governance, networks, culture, and institutions developed through past examples of successful ventures. There is a very good coherence between these two frameworks, and in fact, further conceptualisations present in the literature depict a similar composition of entrepreneurial ecosystems (e.g. Cohen 2006; Isenberg 2011; Brown and Mason 2017; Bertello et al. 2022). Whilst some of these elements cannot be manifested by a particular actor, but rather show the ecosystem's context – i.e. institutions, networks, culture – the remaining ones embody more specific actor types, as discussed in the next sections.

These actor types find their equivalents in university entrepreneurial ecosystems at a sub-system level represented by parent university, business incubators and science parks, technology transfer offices, investors, management team talent, other universities and industry (Prokop and Thompson 2023; Prokop 2021). A few of these actors go beyond what Stam's (2015) or Spigel's (2017) frameworks capture, for example there is little recognition that ecosystems are connected and may jointly and frequently across distant geographies produce entrepreneurial outcomes (Prokop 2021). Similarly, university entrepreneurial ecosystems account for industry networks that do not represent customers or suppliers, but rather past collaborators (Prokop and Thompson 2023) that enable academic founders to gain their initial commercial acumen and informal advisors to discuss application of university inventions with.

Some actors in the ecosystem may be difficult to identify empirically owing to their informal character, such as dealmakers or mentors, but these are critical components of ecosystems (Spigel and Harrison 2018). In fact, ecosystems produce their own actors as they evolve, where past entrepreneurs may recycle into new roles expanding the ecosystem's composition, e.g. as advisors or mentors, or by joining boards of directors (Brown and Mason 2017), employing their experience and networks. University entrepreneurial ecosystems observe this with serial academic entrepreneurs, who are found to contribute to the development of entrepreneurial culture, mentor their departmental colleagues in entrepreneurship, and bring in the entrepreneurial networks developed whilst building academic spinouts (Shane 2004). In evolutionary terms, these can be considered as waves (Berggren and Dahlstrand 2009), with each one strengthening the ecosystem by the addition of new networks and recycled roles.

Whilst most of the university entrepreneurial ecosystem actors could be found in the vicinity of its anchor tenant, for example, business incubators, science parks, technology transfer offices, spinout companies, academic founders, students and mentors, other actors may be less proximate, some of which may only be located in different regions and cities. For example, it is well known that business finance tends to concentrate in particular locations (Klagge and Martin 2005; Huggins and Prokop 2014), making its accessibility difficult, but not impossible if strong connections are developed (Prokop 2021). Similarly, management talent for high technology firms can be typically found in places that host such clusters, e.g. Silicon Valley, Helsinki, or Cambridge/ Oxfordshire. Although investors may not require physical presence and frequent engagement with their investees, management teams do, and geography may make access to such talent more difficult, especially for more peripheral university entrepreneurial ecosystems (Prokop 2021). Consequently, it is important to recognise that geography is an important dimension of university entrepreneurial ecosystems, and when needed, university entrepreneurial ecosystems develop connections to distant actors, making them cross local boundaries and embedded in the wider entrepreneurial ecosystems literature (e.g. Roundy et al. 2018; Spigel 2017).

Compositions of Coexisting Ecosystems

University entrepreneurial ecosystems generate academic spinout companies as key high-growth high-technology ventures. However, other entrepreneurial outputs related to universities, such as student or staff startups, cannot be discounted, especially as these occur in greater volumes, although typically as less technologically advanced or capital intensive (e.g. academic consultancies). Some scholars brand all university-linked ventures under the umbrella of university entrepreneurial ecosystems (Huang-Saad et al. 2017; Hallam et al. 2017; Theodoraki et al. 2018), as these firms, in some circumstances, may transform to very successful enterprises, evidence of which can be observed from corporate US giants such as Facebook and Google, both of which had very modest origins at university campuses (Harvard and Stanford respectively).

However, it is possible that the university entrepreneurial ecosystem could have a parallel campus entrepreneurial ecosystem (Miller and Acs 2017), focused on student entrepreneurship, one that operates separately from academic spinout focus, yet with the same leading anchor tenant – the university. The emerging literature shows three distinct strands that are broadly branded as university entrepreneurial ecosystems that require disentangling for conceptual clarity. These either show clear distinctions, i.e. a university entrepreneurial ecosystem focused on academic spinouts (Lahikainen et al. 2019; Prokop 2021, 2022; Prokop and Thompson 2023), or a campus entrepreneurial ecosystem focused on student/graduate ventures (Miller and Acs 2017; Hallam et al. 2014; Secundo et al. 2021), or include all types of university-related entrepreneurship in the university entrepreneurial ecosystem concept (e.g. Theodoraki et al. 2018) – on occasion making these no different from broader local entrepreneurial ecosystems (Link and Sarala 2019). Since the entrepreneur is the focus in entrepreneurial ecosystems (Stam 2015), the academic spinout or student venture focus clearly identifies two ecosystems: the university entrepreneurial ecosystem, with an academic entrepreneur, and the campus entrepreneurial ecosystem, with a student entrepreneur.

There is good evidence for their parallel yet individual character, given their different focus in terms of outputs and possibly actors (e.g. universities do not mandate another unit to recruit external management team talent nor protect the intellectual property of student ventures) (Wright et al. 2017), but also importantly culture and institutions governing each of them (Miller and Acs 2017). Consequently, their compositions appear to stress different actors. For example, university entrepreneurial ecosystems in order to form and

develop spinout companies tend to rely on a technology transfer office, industry networks, venture capitalists, business angels, and external experienced
management talent (Prokop 2022; Lahikainen et al. 2019). In contrast, campus
entrepreneurial ecosystems highlight the key role of entrepreneurial education
and actors that participate in such activities – e.g. mentors, successful entrepreneurs, and alumni, as well as accelerators and other incubation programmes
(Miller and Acs 2017; Hallam et al. 2014), which assist students or graduates
in developing their ventures (Breznitz and Zhang 2019). Incidentally, these are
also the actors that appear least important (at least in a direct role of incubation) to academic spinouts (e.g. Hewitt-Dundas 2015; Prokop et al. 2019), but
osmotically may leak in entrepreneurial talent, human capital, and networks
into the university entrepreneurial ecosystem. The campus entrepreneurial
ecosystem's actors to a much lesser extent focus on further development, not
to mention longer term nurturing as in the case of academic spinouts (Prokop
2021) closely tied to their university parents through equity. Whilst models of
campus entrepreneurial ecosystem account for a wider set of actors that include
investors (Miller and Acs 2017), the character of student ventures, many not
based on technology, and academic spinouts based on university generated
intellectual property, makes the nature of their financing and required support
very different.

It is important to note that whilst the university as a central university entrepreneurial ecosystem actor exercises a degree of control over the formation of
academic spinouts, it does not have the same influence with regards to student
startup activity. The reason for this is the aforementioned lack of underlying
university intellectual property forming the basis of venture creation (Breznitz
and Zhang 2019). In fact, the research endowment of a university is only
related to the formation of academic spinouts (Marzocchi et al. 2019), further
stressing this crucial ecosystem distinction. However, it is vital to recognise
that some of these firms may be based on ideas or solutions developed at the
university, but, crucially, not owned by the university.

What remains clear is that the literature clearly separates ecosystems
focused on academic spinout companies and those that focus on student enterprises (Wright et al. 2017; Breznitz and Zhang 2019; Miller and Acs 2019;
Prokop 2021; Prokop and Thompson 2023), even though both may occupy
the same physical space and reside at the same university campus, and coexist
in a unique form of symbiotic relationship. The idiosyncratic identities of the
university entrepreneurial ecosystem and campus entrepreneurial ecosystem
are manifested by their individual compositions and configurations. A parallel
ecosystem paradox is explored further in Chapter 5. Importantly though,
it shows how university entrepreneurial ecosystem actors exist separately
from campus entrepreneurial ecosystems, or, as is the case with incubators

and accelerators, co-exist but perform different functions for each parallel ecosystem.

UNIVERSITY

Leadership in an entrepreneurial ecosystem can be represented by actors that guide the direction of ecosystem development and activities, and can be captured by a single entity or more typically by a group of actors organised towards shared goals (Stam and Van de Ven 2021), for example a formalised group of startups or small businesses within a particular sector. In the case of university entrepreneurial ecosystems, the leadership role is played by the university. Having this key role means that universities bear multiple responsibilities. These include the establishment or co-founding of key actors, such as technology transfer offices (which may develop high levels of autonomy when operating as external private sector organisations), business incubators and science parks (both often as part of local multi-partner effort), seed funds (for example university challenge funds in the UK), or even sizeable venture capital funds, such as University of Michigan's MINTS (Huang-Saad et al. 2017).

At the same time, the university is the institution where the first stage of academic spinout lifecycle begins – i.e. research, acting as a pre-formation incubator for research projects that may in the future become disclosures and on the basis of which academic spinout companies will be formed. Furthermore, universities attract, accumulate, and develop academic talent, starting from students ending at faculty. These expansive functions of universities make them unique ecosystem-generating actors that are critical to the perseverance and sustainability of university entrepreneurial ecosystems, and potentially wider locally based entrepreneurial ecosystems (Wadee and Padayachee 2017; Nkusi et al. 2020).

Moreover, universities are also places where prospective academic founders become influenced by their unique cultures and institutions, as well as access to networks that may stimulate establishing companies. As such, universities are microcosms of their regions, and a powerful force for economic development.

Some studies suggest that university business schools should act as key internal resources for academic entrepreneurship (Wright et al. 2009) or hubs of campus entrepreneurial ecosystems (Allahar and Sookram 2019), being parts of universities that find it more natural to engage and promote entrepreneurial activity, and run entrepreneurship education (Breznitz and Zhang 2019), and where no such activity takes place locally, these could play key roles in building ecosystems to transform local economies. In fact, universities are often captured as anchor tenants that are capable of organising or starting up a local place-based entrepreneurial ecosystem rather than hosting one of their own (e.g. Wadee and Padayachee 2017; Nkusi et al. 2020). Consequently, the university is portrayed as a critical and transformative actor, one that also faces multiple pressures owing to the scale of economic development and revitalisation expected of it.

TECHNOLOGY TRANSFER OFFICE

Whilst the key university role in academic entrepreneurship is often portrayed through the presence and activity of the technology transfer office, its remit of activities is very specifically focused on knowledge transfer. Technology transfer offices are not solely devoted to academic spinouts, be it through identification of disclosures or supporting spinouts after they become incorporated, but also dealing with the licensing of university technologies (e.g. patents) to industry. Technology transfer offices participate in university intellectual property protection through patent applications (Siegel et al. 2004), decide on a particular commercialisation route, whether licensing or spinout formation (Alexander and Martin 2013), recruit management talent for spinout companies (BVCA/Library House 2005), identify funding opportunities – consultancy work for faculty or donations – to support knowledge transfer (Fitzgerald and Cunningham 2016), in particular applying for grants to fund prototype development (Prokop 2017), offer initial seed funding for academic spinouts (Gubitta et al. 2016), and build connections with venture capitalists (Franklin et al. 2001) or other university TTOs (Lockett et al. 2003).

This plethora of activities signifies a very engaged role of technology transfer officers, yet it differs across the higher education sector. Markman et al. (2005) identify three types of technology transfer offices: (a) traditional university department; (b) independent non-profit research foundation; and (c) independent for-profit commercial arms of universities, with the last one being the most capable of stimulating entrepreneurial activity, given its strong financial motive. However, this is not always the case, and the internal university departments can perform equally well, depending on their level of resources and organisation (Prokop 2021).

The academic entrepreneurship literature shows distinctly different engagement of technology transfer offices across spinout company development stages. At pre-formation its roles are standardised in performing administrative functions (Shane 2004; Macho-Stadler et al. 2007), but generally not found to be associated as determinants of spinout numbers (Prokop and Thompson 2023; Clarysse, Tartari and Salter 2011). Quite surprisingly, technology transfer offices play more engaged roles at post-formation in supporting spinout company growth, for example by supporting companies in applying for grants and other types of funding. As such their post-formation support is significantly associated with spinout success (Prokop et al. 2019).

SPINOUT COMPANY

The key output of university entrepreneurial ecosystem, the star actor – an academic spinout company – is also an actor that contributes to building the ecosystem. First, each spinout that was formed or failed to start up, attracted funding or was unable to find finance, grew, stagnated or declined, developed a product or was unsuccessful at doing so, survived for many years or closed, offers a unique portfolio of experience, entrepreneurship learning opportunities, stories/examples, practice, and human capital development. It contributes to the development of the university entrepreneurial ecosystem's composition, when key actors are observed to be missing. It allows the university entrepreneurial ecosystem actors, and especially the university, to identify performance outcomes and calibrate the ecosystem's composition and configuration to achieve better regional economic development outcomes.

Second, academic spinouts contribute to the development of local clusters; as such they enable knowledge to spill over beyond the university entrepreneurial ecosystem (Benneworth and Charles 2005; Garnsey and Heffernan 2005), with its value captured in a wider regional entrepreneurial ecosystem.

Third, academic spinout companies whether successful or failed add to entrepreneurial recycling (Spigel and Vinodrai 2021), releasing ideas, human capital, experienced management talent, and academic founders, who could all find new roles as mentors, advisors, angel investors, or success stories, or refresh their old roles with new ventures. This is especially critical in terms of serial academic entrepreneurs, who may have a large portfolio of disclosures and patented intellectual property to convert into products or services through the vehicle of an academic spinout company. Consequently, spinout companies are both outputs and inputs in university entrepreneurial ecosystems, with each failed enterprise giving invaluable level of feedback for ecosystem calibration.

FACULTY

Academic staff are a critical resource in a university entrepreneurial ecosystem. They nurture research ideas, produce knowledge, and are a pool of potential entrepreneurs, the focus of university entrepreneurial ecosystems. In many instances, they are the talent hired by academic spinouts to conduct consultancy, contract or collaborative research that a spinout company cannot perform without access to sophisticated lab equipment and human capital. Whilst not all academics become entrepreneurs, given a diversity of career goals and the specificity of each scientific field in terms of ability to generate commercially applicable knowledge (Shane 2004), most academic research is conducted collaboratively, with knowledge being built over time and cumulatively, making all academics participants in forming conditions at university entrepreneurial ecosystems for spinout opportunities.

This makes academic entrepreneurs a unique subset that is capable of identifying commercial application or viability of knowledge. In fact, Huang-Saad et al. (2017) identify four types of academic inventors: (a) the purest scientist that does not engage with academic entrepreneurship; (b) the contributor, who is not ready or willing to lead an entrepreneurship project, but may assist with one led by someone else; (c) the apprentice who has no entrepreneurial experience, but is willing to start the journey and learn; and (d) the inevitable entrepreneur, a small proportion of faculty that regardless of barriers will engage in academic entrepreneurship, even if the university entrepreneurial ecosystem is undeveloped or poorly calibrated.

Whilst the perception may be that many successful academic entrepreneurs belong to the last type, e.g. star scientists (Gilsing et al. 2010; Lawton Smith et al. 2008; Toole and Czarnitzky 2007), in reality many are either contributors or apprentices, suggesting a rather large pool of potential entrepreneurs. As with the ACE programme at University of Texas at San Antonio devoted to students (Hallam et al. 2014), entrepreneurial skills and mindset can also be developed among academics with appropriately designed educational programmes (Grimaldi et al. 2011; Sansone et al. 2021), indicating a potentially powerful pool of entrepreneurial talent at well-calibrated university entrepreneurial ecosystems. Therefore, faculty are present at all stages of development of academic spinout ventures manifested by distinct roles and types of engagements.

STUDENTS

Whilst students constitute pools of potential entrepreneurs in campus university entrepreneurial ecosystems, their engagement in academic entrepreneurship of university entrepreneurial ecosystems is significant, even though typically not as entrepreneurs. At early stages of academic spinout formation, business school students may be engaged in feasibility studies conducted for early-stage ventures, working on projects as part of their degree programmes (Huggins, Prokop, Steffenson, Johnston and Clifton 2014). Such work engages students in practical application of their skills and knowledge, developing their entrepreneurial skills, but also supports startups, in particular, academic spinout companies (Rasmussen and Wright 2015; Walsh et al. 2021). There is evidence that graduate students may be more directly engaged in the formation of academic spinouts, either as co-founders (Hayter et al. 2017) or employed to continue advanced research on technology development in the spinout companies (Hayter 2016). As such, they may at times play roles that are equal to academic founders, even though alongside them. This partnership is potentially deeper, where students are found to also encourage faculty to establish spinout ventures in the first place (Hayter 2016).

At later stages students are found to remain in spinout companies, at times becoming CEOs and leading the company development (Hayter et al. 2017), often offering complementary skills to academic founders (Walsh et al. 2021). In fact, whilst the role of academic founders may diminish in the later stages of academic spinout development, for example when the key technology is developed or the technology transfer office has a specific policy on their engagement (Prokop 2017), it is found that students continue with academic spinouts (Boh et al. 2016). This is not necessarily a surprising finding, but it is important to understand students as actors of university entrepreneurial ecosystems, since academic founders rarely vacate their academic positions. This also suggests that academic spinout companies may offer career opportunities to students, especially those pursuing advanced degrees (Boh et al. 2016), whilst being merely a career enhancing feature for faculty.

Overall, students constitute a malleable human capital whose intellectual and professional development trajectory may be influenced by academic founders and university. At the same time, they may play a part in determining academic spinout formation, indicating their critical role in university entrepreneurial ecosystems.

INCUBATOR FACILITIES

Incubation takes different forms: through traditional business incubators, accelerators, or science parks. Whilst incubation is designated as a critical process for any early-stage venture, as it helps to protect firms from failure (Carayannis and von Zedtwitz 2005) and offers space (Grimaldi and Grandi 2005), networks and mentors (Wynarczyk and Raine 2005), and other services to build a business, academic spinout companies are not found to use business incubators (Hewitt-Dundas 2015), nor are these found to be important to academic spinout company formation (Lockett and Wright 2005; Fini et al. 2011; Salvador and Rolfo 2011) or survival (Prokop et al. 2019). The key reason behind this is the fact that the vast majority of academic spinouts incubate in university departments (Hewitt-Dundas 2015), even though, especially in the UK, many incubators, including science parks, are either owned or co-owned by universities.

Although this may initially suggest that business incubators should not be part of university entrepreneurial ecosystems, especially as they are more prominently featuring in campus entrepreneurial ecosystems (Miller and Acs 2017), they play less obvious roles in the academic spinout lifecycle. As facilities that gather entrepreneurial talent, reflected in multiple diverse businesses using incubator services, they build networks that through the university entrepreneurial ecosystem are made available for academic spinout companies. These networks may offer connections to experienced entrepreneurs, management talent, or even to investors (Prokop 2021). Furthermore, science parks, frequently located at university campuses, may host well-established firms (Tamasy 2007), which could act as important contacts as potential customers, suppliers, or research and development collaborators for academic spinouts. Incubators are found especially important to poorly developed entrepreneurial ecosystems (Prokop 2021), where the density of actors may be lacking. As such, they could infuse a critical density of connections into struggling ecosystems, given their extensive networks, making them vital hubs of sustainable university entrepreneurial ecosystems (Theodoraki et al. 2018).

MANAGEMENT TALENT

The key expertise of academic founders is linked to their technology. It is found that academic spinouts with management teams that include individuals with business skills or prior startup experience are more successful (Grandi and Grimaldi 2003; Criaco et al. 2014). Such complementarity of skills and experience allows the external management talent and academic founders to perform heterogeneous functions at academic spinouts, with the former focused on building a business typically as a chief executive officer, whilst the latter is devoted to the development of the key technology as a chief technology officer.

This specialist functional approach is found to be a key factor contributing to a spinout's growth (Vohora et al. 2004). It indicates the importance of diverse skills being present in management teams of academic spinouts (Visintin and Pittino 2014), but also motivations that may influence the spinout's performance (Civera et al. 2024). Furthermore, a good management team is important to attract venture capital funding (Wright et al. 2006), with an experienced management individual indicating the spinout's credibility and commercial focus (Hayter 2016), but also because the individual already had links with specific investors (Gubitta et al. 2016). Furthermore, external management talent typically brings in extensive networks to an academic spinout company that are critical to its growth (Wennberg et al. 2011). For example, these networks may include patent lawyers, accountants, or experts in manufacturing (Hayter 2016).

Typically, academic spinouts recruit external management talent prior to company formation (Prokop 2021), often to pass the responsibility over company development from a technology transfer officer to an experienced professional. At later stages, management team composition may change, when academic spinouts need to scale up, reflecting changing requirements for leadership and management experience. This late-stage dynamism is captured in shareholder networks which actively readapt to ensure spinout success (Prokop and Kitagawa 2022).

INVESTORS

The core problem of academic spinouts is lack of resources (Prokop 2023), being a company created from a university environment with an undeveloped technology and its key founder already having a strong commitment to current employment. Financial resources are critical, as spinouts would otherwise be unable to develop novel advanced technologies into marketable products or services. The key asset of a spinout company is its technology or knowledge, which if protected by patents may attract venture capital investment (Siegel et al. 2007).

Consequently, academic spinouts are considerably better than other types of firms in attracting injections of venture finance, with 37.5% of all UK spinouts in receipt of venture capital-type funding in 2014 (Hewitt-Dundas 2015). UK data (employed in Prokop et al. 2019) show that in a 3-year period for academic spinouts born between 2011 and 2013 approximately 25.1% were in receipt of venture capital by 2014, whilst for those registered in 2013, 15.0% received venture capital by 2014. In comparison, venture capital-type investments in the UK in 2021 supported 949 companies (BVCA 2022), when just the new births of firms in 2020 accounted for 333,000 companies (ONS 2022), equating to 0.3% of UK firms (of course, venture capitalists might consider a wider stock of firms than just newly born ones). It is clear that academic spinouts have a much stronger likelihood of attracting finance that would accelerate their growth, indicating the highly successful prospects expected by venture capital community.

When the academic spinout is at pre-formation stage or just established, the funding is typically skewed towards the seed stage, potentially research grants; much of that financing tends to be provided by well-endowed universities or research councils (to develop the technology) (Prokop 2021). Seed funding is considered credibility signalling by the venture capital community (Wright et al. 2006), increasing the likelihood of investment. At later stages venture capital firms tend to dominate in spinout financing, as they typically stay with firms for a longer period of time, with some specialised venture capital firms nurturing (i.e. investing in multiple rounds) academic spinouts even for 15 years (Prokop 2021) before exiting the investment.

THE EVOLVING MODEL OF UNIVERSITY ENTREPRENEURIAL ECOSYSTEMS

These core actors form diverse types of university entrepreneurial ecosystem compositions that serve spinouts and evolve together with them, specifically pointing towards actors that play early-stage roles, such as technology transfer officers, academic staff, incubation facilities, and universities, and later-stage roles involving predominantly external management talent and investors. Given this evolutionary complexity, especially related to re-structuring of the importance of actors across academic spinout lifecycle, I build an evolving model of the university entrepreneurial ecosystem (Figure 4.1) that takes on a perspective of a spinout company. The model integrates discussions contained in this chapter to present how the composition of the university entrepreneurial ecosystem changes with the stages of spinout company development.

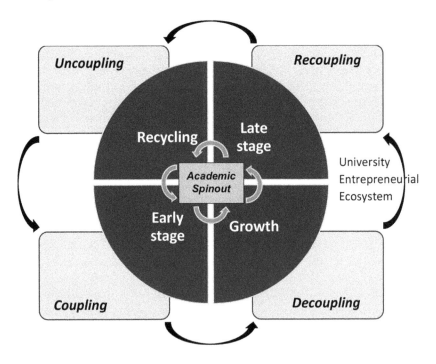

Figure 4.1   *The evolving model of university entrepreneurial ecosystem and spinout lifecycle*

At the early stages of the academic spinout company the key actors involved relate to protype testing, identifying the opportunity by consulting industry contacts, building a management team that has commercial experience and includes academic founders – by employing networks of the technology transfer office or university business incubator, hiring students or other human capital to either help identify market feasibility or develop the technology. More successful academic spinouts may attract their initial seed funding, or grants to help develop a prototype. Importantly, if the spinout company is a result of research collaboration between academics working at different institutions, access to actors enlarges, as multiple university entrepreneurial ecosystems become connected by such spinouts. Crucially, this stage represents a *coupling* process, where actors are being connected for the first time to the academic spinout.

During the growth period, academic spinouts accumulate network capital (Huggins 2010) and the composition of the university entrepreneurial actors they require starts changing. For example, the management team becomes firmly important in driving the company's development, whilst the academic founder starts to become less relevant, potentially transitioning away from academic spinout and back to original university employment. The orientation of company activities changes from technology development to developing the business, potentially initiating first sales. As the spinout attracts venture capital investment, it begins to attract more human capital, potentially from non-proximate places. This period represents a *decoupling* process, where an academic spinout develops its commercial credibility through a gradual detachment from the university parent. At this point, the spinout company may also change its location from a university department to a proximate but more officially existing office space (e.g. incubator or traditional office).

When academic spinouts enter the late stage, their needs mature, as reflected in a different composition of university entrepreneurial ecosystem required. The technology transfer office continues to support academic spinout but in a responsive way, listening to the needs of an academic spinout. Two key actors of such a spinout company are the management team and the venture capital investor. Whilst the former may change to reflect scaled-up operations for an experienced CEO, the latter continues to invest increasing amounts eyeing exit opportunities, either as the sale of the spinout company or an initial public offering. At the same time, a dynamic restructuring of shareholder networks is taking place (Prokop and Kitagawa 2022), to reflect the greater level of demands of a spinout company in order to increase its exit value (Bonardo et al. 2011). As some of the key actor types remain the same, but not the individual actors, this stage represents a *recoupling* process, where the spinout company reconnects actors that will be important in the future.

Finally, late-stage academic spinouts may either achieve an exit or at any point potentially fail, entering a recycling period. At this point the accumulated networks, experience, learning, skills, etc., are released back to the university entrepreneurial ecosystem. Many actors will become more knowledgeable about entrepreneurship, but some will return in new roles, for example as mentors or angel investors. Academic founders that were particularly successful may become serial entrepreneurs with their next ventures. The university entrepreneurial ecosystem benefits from the developed human capital retained in the ecosystem (if further outputs are generated to employ it) as well as institutional development, in particular with the success stories championing entrepreneurial activity (Spigel 2017), or failure stories feeding back instructions for better calibration of the ecosystem. Spinout recycling represents an *uncoupling* process, where actors involved in the academic spinout venture are freed of their responsibilities to that company, but continue their part in the university entrepreneurial ecosystem.

CONCLUSION

Not all university entrepreneurial ecosystems follow the same composition, which critically may influence how many academic spinout companies are generated (Prokop 2022). However, even if actors are not available in the university's vicinity, ecosystem builders need to recognise that spatial boundaries such as administrative limits of a city or town (Schäfer 2021) cannot define a university entrepreneurial ecosystem, as discussed in subsequent chapters. The missing actors may be available elsewhere and require the development of connections to integrate them into a university entrepreneurial ecosystem.

Additionally, it is important to note that university entrepreneurial ecosystem actors change their roles with the lifecycle of a spinout company. As a result, each spinout company requires a different composition that aides its current stage of development. In other words, university entrepreneurial ecosystem actors become activated and deactivated according to the needs of spinout companies, but crucially shape the evolving composition of the university entrepreneurial ecosystem.

5.   Levels of ecosystems

Much of the literature on entrepreneurial ecosystems has assumed that these are cohesive place-based constructs (Spigel 2022; Schäfer 2021) that encompass an administrative place, such as Waterloo (Spigel and Vinodrai 2021), Toulouse (Gueguen et al. 2021), Bangalore or Tokyo (Kapturkiewicz 2022), reflecting actors and elements that are well connected and spatially contained. The emerging evidence, primarily drawn from studying university entrepreneurial ecosystems (e.g. Prokop 2021; Prokop and Thompson 2023), but also wider entrepreneurial ecosystem research (Spigel 2022), shows a more complex reality, with a possibility for poor connectedness, clustering, sub-ecosystems, and trans-spatiality. This theoretical incongruence requires systematisation of the organisation of ecosystems.

The purpose of this chapter is to respond to this need by proposing a taxonomy of ecosystems, which explains the unique existence of university entrepreneurial ecosystems and recognises that other distinctive sub-ecosystems may also be present, such as technology- or sector-based. It then explores how these coexist by proposing alternative explanations through three models: hierarchical, nested, and hybrid.

IS THERE MORE THAN ONE ECOSYSTEM IN A PLACE?

As established in previous chapters, there is clear evidence that each place, whether a city, city-region (e.g. Reading; Godley et al. 2021), or a wider administrative (or virtual) region, holds multiple entrepreneurial ecosystems in a form of sub-ecosystems. It emerges that there are levels of ecosystems (Prokop and Thompson 2023), with an aggregate place-based entrepreneurial ecosystem (PBEE) bounded by administrative geography (Schäfer 2021), predominantly at the scale of locality such as a city or town, and a range of entrepreneurial sub-ecosystems (ESEs), with the attention devoted in this book to university entrepreneurial ecosystems (UEEs), but recognising the existence of other types that develop around a particular sector or technology. Each PBEE contains multiple sub-ecosystems, predominantly university entrepreneurial ecosystems. However, the literature also suggests sectoral entrepreneurial ecosystems (SEEs) (e.g. Berman et al. 2022), technology entrepreneurial ecosystems (TEEs) (Sussan and Acs 2017), and business incubator entrepreneurial ecosystems (BIEE) (e.g. Van Rijnsoever 2020). These multiple types of entrepreneurial sub-ecosystems indicate a co-existence of multiple cohesive sub-networks within each place-based entrepreneurial ecosystem, as such indicating a possibility to delineate parallel sub-ecosystems.

Theoretically, this is an important recognition, a first step towards organising understanding of the concept of entrepreneurial ecosystems. It comes as no surprise that there is some order of aggregation built into the concept, with regional entrepreneurial ecosystems, place-based, and sub-ecosystems forming at least three core levels. Given that much of the literature focuses on cities, the latter two levels are this chapter's theoretical focus.

Each place hosting more than one sub-ecosystem questions the primary argument of the cohesiveness of entrepreneurial ecosystems (Spigel 2022), revealing more complexity than has been attributed to them. Whilst not necessarily suggesting a complete disconnect, network theory indicates that sub-networks are naturally occurring concentrations of connections between actors (Zane and DeCarolis 2016). This may be a result of homophilious characteristics of actors that bring them together towards cohesive actions, as such suggesting that cohesiveness is still part of this multiple parallel ecosystems reality (Spigel 2022), just manifested at a sub-ecosystem level.

The presence of multiple ecosystems or network clusters (i.e. sub-networks) is not surprising, but it calls into question the empirical and methodological works that operated in theoretical 'liberty', equating sub-ecosystems with place-based entrepreneurial ecosystems. This chapter tries to organise these works (as shown below) by illustrating the taxonomy of entrepreneurial ecosystems.

THE TAXONOMY OF ECOSYSTEMS

The emerging research trying to distinguish between multiple types of entrepreneurial ecosystems has presented a number of frameworks and conceptualisations that at times stand against empirical research published. For example, Spigel and Harrison (2018) suggest that ecosystems are technology, e.g. digital (Sussan and Acs 2017), rather than sector focused, yet many empirical studies clearly show the existence of sectoral entrepreneurial ecosystems, e.g. fintech (Frimanslund 2022; Alaassar et al. 2022; Koroleva 2022), sport (Ratten and Thompson 2020), automotive and ICT (Focacci and Kirov 2021), biotechnology (Auerswald and Dani 2017), or life sciences (Alvedalen and Carlsson 2021). These distinctions are made to try and portray the entrepreneurial ecosystems as a unique concept different from clusters or innovation systems, yet the empirical evidence suggests that entrepreneurial ecosystem theory builds on those works – it is an intellectual evolution. It is difficult to dismiss the contribution of studies that do not follow the 'uniqueness', 'separateness', and 'independence' of the entrepreneurial ecosystem concept, as they contribute new evidence to develop this theory, which – as with clusters and innovation systems concepts – may evolve (Autio et al. 2018). At the same time, the crux of the entrepreneurial ecosystems literature does not characterise sectoral ecosystems as a type of ecosystem. Whilst technology-based ecosystems (Sussan and Acs 2017) are recognised, these end up focusing along sectoral lines (e.g. Ratten and Thompson 2020).

These issues are important, as sectors may exhibit different spatial patterns, either completely concentrated in a place or scattered across a wider area, as observed from clusters such as Helsinki or Silicon Valley, respectively. Recognising sectoral entrepreneurial ecosystems is therefore important to understanding the organisation of place-based entrepreneurial ecosystems.

Another critical problem with the typology of entrepreneurial ecosystems is that they may merely focus on their temporality or evolution (Brown and Mason 2017; Spigel and Harrison 2018; Autio et al. 2018), but contribute very little to recognising and understanding two (or more) entrepreneurial ecosystems at the same (or different) stage of development. Whilst it is critical to appreciate that each unique place-based entrepreneurial ecosystem may exhibit a different stage of development influencing its configuration, completeness and ability to deliver specific outputs (Brown and Mason 2017; Kapturkiewicz 2022), it remains unclear how ecosystems relate to each other. Consequently, focusing on the temporal dimension still lacks the theoretical complexity needed to develop the concept of entrepreneurial ecosystems (Muñoz et al. 2022).

As such, I argue here that any typology of entrepreneurial ecosystems needs to account for the spatial organisation of entrepreneurial sub-ecosystems (Frimanslund 2022), which individually, fully or partially contribute to place-based or local constructs presented in a myriad of empirical studies. Whilst references to spatial aspects of entrepreneurial ecosystems have been made (Brown and Mason 2017; Pita et al. 2021), these have often been cursory at best and tended to equate multiple spatial scales, instead of carefully differentiating between them. Consequently, an entrepreneurial ecosystem of a country becomes empirically equal to one of a city, ignoring the contextual factors such as institutions, networks and governance systems that are multiscalar and different across spatial scales (Pike et al. 2015). Again, this approach risks missing the local context and complexity in favour of parsimonious theoretical development (Muñoz et al. 2022), especially when entrepreneurship has a strong local character (Brown and Mason 2017; Malecki 2018). The taxonomy presented below shows that entrepreneurial ecosystems or entrepreneurial sub-ecosystems may exist across multiple places (Frimanslund 2022).

In what follows I present three key models that recognise different types of entrepreneurial ecosystems: (a) hierarchical; (b) nested; and (c) hybrid.

THE HIERARCHICAL ECOSYSTEM MODEL

One of the ways in which entrepreneurial ecosystems are organised reflects trans-spatiality and the utilisation of hierarchical structuring of ecosystems. This is reflected in the functioning of the entrepreneurial sub-ecosystems, which exist across multiple place-based entrepreneurial ecosystems. Such spatial arrangement enables them to connect actors available in different places, where some ecosystemic elements may be present (for example, investors, accelerators, entrepreneurial talent, dealmakers, etc.), in the absence of locally available ones. This trans-spatial organisation enables entrepreneurial sub-ecosystems to access resources and tap into institutional arrangements present in different places (Pike et al. 2015) – strengthening each sub-ecosystem. Place offers a strategic level of infrastructure, resources and institutions that entrepreneurial sub-ecosystems access in this hierarchical setup. In turn, entrepreneurial sub-ecosystems represent an operational level with actors that cluster within and across places.

In the hierarchical ecosystem model, entrepreneurial sub-ecosystems venture outside their own operational level in structuring their activities to access strategic level elements present in other places. This model has been observed among university entrepreneurial ecosystems (Prokop 2021), with especially the more peripheral or locally less developed university entrepreneurial ecosystems following the hierarchical model to resolve their local place-based entrepreneurial ecosystem limitations, enabling them access to entrepreneurial talent or investors available elsewhere.

The hierarchical ecosystem model represents ecosystem organisation that overcomes insufficient development of local place-based entrepreneurial ecosystems or its development that does not serve a particular entrepreneurial sub-ecosystem. For example, if a place-based entrepreneurial ecosystem is not organised around any particular sector, perhaps owing to limited sectoral specialisation, but an existing university entrepreneurial ecosystem forms spinout companies that sectorally exhibit specific needs – like nanotechnology, materials science, biotechnology, or life sciences companies – that university entrepreneurial ecosystem will lack the necessary ecosystem elements to serve its diverse ventures. University entrepreneurial ecosystems in these circumstances would develop connections outside of their place-based entrepreneurial ecosystems to access strategic-level ecosystem elements to support ventures they generate, by building presence in place-based entrepreneurial ecosystems equipped with strategic level elements responsive to advanced technology demands.

Figure 5.1 depicts the hierarchical ecosystem model. It delineates the strategic (represented with continuous lines) and operational (portrayed with

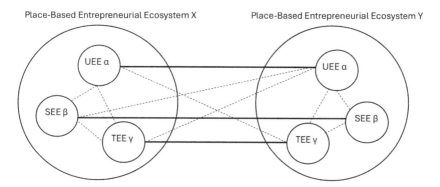

Place-Based Entrepreneurial Ecosystem X Place-Based Entrepreneurial Ecosystem Y

Figure 5.1 *The hierarchical ecosystem model*

dotted lines) levels that entrepreneurial sub-ecosystems utilise by employing a trans-spatial organisation. In essence, entrepreneurial sub-ecosystems illustrated in this framework (*UEE α, SEE β, TEE γ*) organise the multiple actor-types and elements across various place-based entrepreneurial ecosystems to achieve completeness, and consequently operational effectiveness. This may include one place-based entrepreneurial ecosystem (e.g. *PBEE Y*) having investors, and business incubators or accelerators, and yet another (e.g. *PBEE X*), a university and technology transfer office that forms spinout companies. At the same time, entrepreneurial sub-ecosystems organised hierarchically may also have internal (at place-based entrepreneurial ecosystem level) connections among them and external connections to entrepreneurial sub-ecosystems of other place-based entrepreneurial ecosystems. However, these connections would not be based on adding new types of actors, rather replicating the types already available to them. In a hierarchical ecosystem model, each entrepreneurial sub-ecosystem would follow this trans-spatial organisation, including sectoral and technological entrepreneurial ecosystems.

THE NESTED ECOSYSTEM MODEL

Given the multiple levels of entrepreneurial ecosystems (Brown and Mason 2017) – national entrepreneurial ecosystems, regional entrepreneurial ecosystems, place-based entrepreneurial ecosystems, and entrepreneurial sub-ecosystems – it remains unsurprising that they may be organised in a nested way, as observed by Spigel (2022) in his study of fintech entrepreneurial ecosystems. In essence, nested ecosystems have a strong place-bounded character. Whilst they do not show trans-spatial organisation, nested ecosystems may have connections to other ecosystems (Prokop and Thompson 2023), whether nested or hierarchical. This place-based and bounded character reflects the parsimonious conceptualisation of entrepreneurial ecosystems seen across multiple studies (e.g. Kapturkiewicz 2022; Spigel and Vinodrai 2021), making it the most familiar framework of ecosystem organisation. Nestedness shows that entrepreneurial sub-ecosystems exist in well-developed place-based entrepreneurial ecosystems that are characterised by strong internal connectedness, even though showing some level of local clustering (Spigel 2022). This clustering along sectoral or technological lines has been observed in multiple studies depicting sectoral entrepreneurial ecosystems or technology entrepreneurial ecosystems, yet not attributing this nature to the specific organisation of an ecosystem.

It is important to recognise that nested ecosystems include university entrepreneurial ecosystems, so long as these are spatially contained in a wider place-based entrepreneurial ecosystem. What this means for university entrepreneurial ecosystems, is that the resources, institutions, and infrastructure they access are locally available, cognitively representing a more uniform – local – context, in which social capital is both larger and stronger, and potentially easier to access. This is especially greater for entrepreneurs (especially academic ones) who have a longer history in the locality owing to cumulative effects of social capital and embeddedness in the institutional arrangements of a place (Schutjens and Volker 2010).

Global cities, such as London, New York, Tokyo, and Beijing, are more likely to host nested university entrepreneurial ecosystems, owing to their high level of developed networks, availability of actors, opportunities, talent, and infrastructure, but also entrepreneurship-friendly institutional context (Sim et al. 2003). In fact, such place-based entrepreneurial ecosystems may contain multiple nested entrepreneurial sub-ecosystems, inclusive of those that are sectorally and technologically focused. Conversely, secondary or smaller cities would be places where nested ecosystems would be less frequently observed, where hierarchical ecosystems are more likely to be present instead.

A nested ecosystem model is presented in Figure 5.2. It depicts a variety of entrepreneurial sub-ecosystems (illustrated here with *UEE α, UEE β, SEE γ, TEE δ* in *PBEE X*; and *UEE ε, SEE ζ, SEE η, TEE θ* in *PBEE Y*) that, whilst being nested in their respective place-based entrepreneurial ecosystems, may also have connections of operational character (depicted with dotted lines) to entrepreneurial sub-ecosystems in other place-based entrepreneurial ecosystems. These external connections are important (Prokop and Thompson 2023), but not critical, as they do not substitute the lack of actor types or elements. Instead, such connections are naturally occurring pipelines connecting entrepreneurial ecosystems and strengthening their nested character with a further variety of actors within actor types already present in these entrepreneurial sub-ecosystems (for example other investors in *PBEE X SEE γ* have access to,

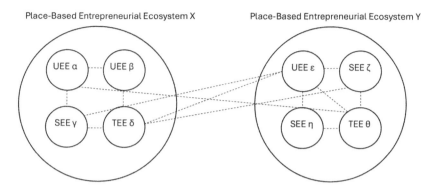

Figure 5.2   The nested ecosystem model

other than those forming *PBEE Y*'s *UEE ε*), by introducing a level of heterophily into such contained and possibly strongly homophilious networks.

THE HYBRID MODEL

Entrepreneurial ecosystems organised in hierarchical and nested ways represent two opposing ends of a spectrum of ecosystem organisation. As such, many entrepreneurial ecosystems would fall in between the two extremes; I denote these as hybrid models. In essence, hybrid organisation represents place-based entrepreneurial ecosystems that contain at least one nested entrepreneurial sub-ecosystem and at least one hierarchical entrepreneurial sub-ecosystem. This could be one nested sectoral entrepreneurial ecosystem – e.g. fintech – and one hierarchical university entrepreneurial ecosystem organised across multiple place-based entrepreneurial ecosystems. Therefore, the hybrid ecosystem model captures the naturally occurring complexity of ecosystems' organisational forms, which cannot fit into parsimonious, but extreme, conceptualisations, such as nested ecosystems.

The hybrid nature enables such place-based entrepreneurial ecosystems to enjoy a greater variety of inputs and entrepreneurial outcomes, as actors within any single hybrid ecosystem form a larger trans-spatial network that has some heterophilious character. At the same time, it is important to note that such network may be susceptible to greater distance (Iacobucci 1994), and a larger presence of structural holes – indicating opportunities (Burt 1992), but also lower levels of cohesiveness, critical to the coordinated functioning of ecosystem actors (Roundy et al. 2018). This may mean that hybrid ecosystems may reveal multiple performance equilibria, with some entrepreneurial sub-ecosystems less developed and underperforming compared with others. Consequently, any entrepreneur's access to ecosystemic elements is dependent on the character of their entrepreneurial sub-ecosystem, with dominant locally available institutions, infrastructure, and actors representing a nested sub-ecosystem, whilst dominant trans-spatial organisation revealing a hierarchical nature.

Figure 5.3 presents a model of a hybrid ecosystem, demonstrating its complex organisation. It is important to note that this is merely illustrative, as hybrid ecosystems represent the broadest range of ecosystems configured in their unique ways. Crucially, hybrid ecosystems contain entrepreneurial sub-ecosystems of nested (e.g. *UEE α, TEE γ* in *PBEE X*; and *SEE η, TEE θ* in *PBEE Y*) and hierarchical character (e.g. *UEE β* and *SEE δ* organised across *PBEE X* and *PBEE Y*), with a minimum of one of each type. Whilst hierarchical type entrepreneurial sub-ecosystems exist trans-spatially (portrayed with a continuous line of strategic connections), both nested and hierarchical entrepreneurial sub-ecosystems may develop intra-place-based entrepreneurial ecosystem and inter-place-based entrepreneurial ecosystem links to other entrepreneurial sub-ecosystems. These connections bring in new actors to supplement already available actor types or elements in these entrepreneurial sub-ecosystems. For example, *UEE β* may have its own dedicated spinout investors in *PBEE Y*, but connect with additional technology-specialised investors that form part of *TEE θ*. Likewise, *UEE α* may already have access to a university business incubator, but for some of its spinouts it may require a more specialised incubator with an accelerator programme devoted to specific technology-based firms present in *TEE θ*. As such, the hybrid model captures a complexity unaccounted for in the extant literature.

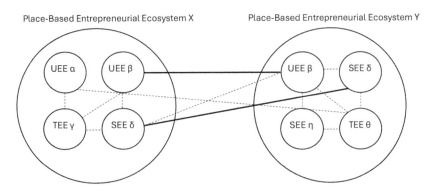

Figure 5.3   The hybrid ecosystem model

CONCLUSION

This chapter constitutes merely one of the efforts to systematise knowledge of entrepreneurial ecosystems. Crucially, it is inspired by observing university entrepreneurial ecosystems, which have received less attention in the mainstream entrepreneurial ecosystems literature. Yet they open up the possibility of looking past the dominant parsimonious perceptions of ecosystems, enabling the positioning of university entrepreneurial ecosystems in complex organisational forms of place-based entrepreneurial ecosystems. The taxonomy of entrepreneurial ecosystems offered here presents a spectrum of forms that ecosystems take, revealing the diverse nature of their organisation. Whilst at the extremes we may observe nested and hierarchical ecosystems, most place-based entrepreneurial ecosystems are actually somewhere in between the two – making them hybrid ecosystems.

Importantly, nested ecosystems can connect to hybrid and hierarchical ones, but these hybrid and hierarchical ones need to be connected to other place-based entrepreneurial ecosystems. Nested ecosystems are the only ones that can exist on their own without external connections. This has been a dominant view of ecosystems, yet it shows potential for a high degree of homophily that may be destructive for ecosystems if these form no external connections.

Hierarchical and hybrid ecosystems do not exist on their own, they require other ecosystems to ensure entrepreneurial sub-ecosystems are organised. They may have connections to each other and to nested ecosystems, but crucially cannot form hierarchies with nested ecosystems, only with hybrids and hierarchical ones. These two models of ecosystems may have a higher chance of achieving sustainable growth, given their openness, and ability to access heterophilious ecosystemic elements.

Whilst it is not the aim of the chapter to offer a final taxonomy of ecosystems, it is hopefully one that draws attention towards recognising the individuality and idiosyncrasy of local entrepreneurial ecosystems. At the very least, it should make it clear why it is so important to recognise and acknowledge the multi-scalar character of entrepreneurial ecosystems in empirical studies.

6. In search of success mechanisms: the entrepreneurial filter

Trying to disentangle the complexity in explaining success of academic spinout companies is an uneasy endeavour. Building on the previous chapters, I try to highlight that a considerable part of success is down to the role of the university entrepreneurial ecosystem functioning as an entrepreneurial filter. In essence, spinout companies undergo multiple rounds of selectivity across the lifecycle of the underlying knowledge, from the initial disclosure stage to final exit. At each such development point the future of the spinout company is determined, with many unable to progress. Building on work in Prokop (2021), I propose entrepreneurial filter theory. It captures a success mechanism built into university entrepreneurial ecosystems, but given limited conceptual attention. Towards the end of the chapter, I elaborate on the wider application of the entrepreneurial filter theory to better understand the success of any company processed through the machinery of place-based entrepreneurial ecosystems.

KNOWLEDGE SPILLOVER THEORY OF ENTREPRENEURSHIP

Investments in generation of new knowledge are key components of endogenous growth theory (Romer 1990), as new knowledge enables productivity increases that go beyond more physically bounded labour and capital components of economic growth equation. As such, governments interested in increasing economic growth need to value their universities, but also private corporations that undertake research and development work. These generate stocks of knowledge that play an important part in contributing to growth. However, the exact mechanism in which knowledge becomes economic growth is more complicated. Knowledge spillover theory of entrepreneurship (Acs et al. 2013) fills this gap by explaining that the key mechanism is entrepreneurial activity. Essentially, new firms are established to profit from the opportunity posed by new knowledge – typically unexplored by incumbent firms. Knowledge presents itself as a strategic and competitive resource of companies (Prokop 2023).

However, new knowledge may not be readily or easily understood by a population of would-be entrepreneurs, nor even available. Universities play here an important role (Audretsch and Lehmann 2005), as these institutions create new knowledge and train the general population in understanding it, essentially improving their absorptive capacity (Cohen and Levinthal 1990). Individuals characterised by higher levels of absorptive capacity are able to acquire and process new knowledge better, potentially becoming sources of entrepreneurship, when they observe the economic opportunities of such knowledge (Acs, Braunerhjelm, Audretsch and Carlsson 2009). Academic spinout companies are one of the key economic mechanisms to process knowledge into economic growth (Acs, Braunerhjelm, Audretsch and Carlsson 2009). This is because they are at the source of knowledge generation, where individuals with sufficient absorptive capacity are available as the original knowledge producers.

It comes as no surprise then that regions with greater levels of investment in new knowledge generation have higher start-up rates (Audretsch and Lehmann 2005), and report greater economic output growth (Acs and Plummer 2005). Further studies confirm that increases in knowledge production would also benefit economically peripheral areas of developed (Acs, Plummer and Sutter 2009) and developing nations (Iftikhar et al. 2020). Consequently, there is a clear theoretical basis to draw policymakers' interest to knowledge and how to generate more of it.

Whilst these are worthy endeavours, it is important to recognise that not all knowledge has potential to contribute to economic growth (Ghio et al. 2015). Some knowledge may have social or other benefits, suggesting that knowledge of economic potential constitutes a proportion of all new knowledge generated (Acs and Plummer 2005). It is also evident that not all individuals with the right level of absorptive capacity end up employing it to create new firms based on knowledge they generated. Moreover, not all of those that identify an entrepreneurial opportunity end up creating a successful venture. Whilst knowledge spillover theory of entrepreneurship holds powerful potential to explain what makes economically successful places and regions do so well, it does not address these two fundamental issues.

The next section focuses on the issue of knowledge conversion capacity that has been captured theoretically under the umbrella term of knowledge filter. It provides a neat explanation of why not all knowledge, even with the right level of human capital, ends up contributing to economic growth.

KNOWLEDGE FILTER

Of all the knowledge generated from research and development activities performed by universities, public research organisations, and private companies (Mueller 2006), a substantial portion of that knowledge remains economically underutilised, for example, a new treatment for a health condition, a new chemical compound, or an econometric model. In other words, any economy's ability to 'process' new knowledge into economic growth is limited by multiple barriers that may be of regulatory (e.g. laws), personal (e.g. motivations) or other character, making this positive economic process (i.e. knowledge spillover theory of entrepreneurship) more difficult (Carlsson et al. 2007; Guerrero and Urbano 2014). This underutilisation is attributed to the knowledge filter, an umbrella term for the aforementioned barriers (Mueller 2006; Carlsson et al. 2007; Shu et al. 2022), explored in this section.

The knowledge filter is more difficult to penetrate with knowledge that is more basic in character, compared with the applied type (Carlsson et al. 2007). Consequently, the knowledge filter is a correction for endogenous growth theory, providing an elegant explanation as to why merely producing knowledge may not lead to economic growth. At the same time, it conceptually interacts with the knowledge spillover theory of entrepreneurship, where entrepreneurship is the solution to all of these barriers that limit the economic potential and utilisation of knowledge.

Importantly, new firms rather than incumbent ones are the prized economic vehicle to deliver economic growth by penetrating the knowledge filter (Acs and Plummer 2005). This is predominantly attributed to the fact that new firms are more effective at converting knowledge, when the economic potential of that knowledge is more uncertain (Audretsch and Belitski 2021). This level of risk offers greater rewards to entrepreneurs, in return incentivising their entrepreneurial efforts compared with employment (Becker 1965). Not all types of firms can play this unique role, as Acs, Plummer and Sutter (2009) point to the importance of technology firms. Crucially, places that can generate more knowledge, such as university towns and cities, observe greater rates of technology entrepreneurship (Audretsch and Lehmann 2005), suggesting that higher education is also an important attribute in explaining the formation of such firms. Given that human capital with greater absorptive capacity can not only appropriate, but also convert, new complex knowledge, this makes absorptive capacity a critical factor in overcoming the knowledge filter (Qian and Jung 2017).

Knowledge filter effects can be reduced by government intervention, where the government revises its policy to reduce barriers to exploiting new knowledge (Shu et al. 2022). This is not very surprising, given that part of the barriers captured by the knowledge filter metaphor are regulatory in nature (Carlsson et al. 2007). It has also been found that venture capital can assist in penetrating the knowledge filter (Padilla-Meléndez et al. 2021), by ensuring that entrepreneurial activity is appropriately supported. However, venture capitalists known to assess raw knowledge are rare and have been focused on academic spinouts (Prokop 2021), where they enter contractual agreements with universities to evaluate their disclosures. Consequently, overcoming barriers to exploit knowledge economically is uneasy and may be best performed at a place where knowledge is actually generated (Acs, Braunerhjelm, Audretsch and Carlsson 2009), resulting in both corporate (with knowledge generated at private companies) and academic spinouts (with knowledge generated at public research organisations or universities).

Whilst entrepreneurship is regarded as an important attribute to penetrate the knowledge filter, little is known about the mechanism in which one piece of knowledge is selected over another, and how such knowledge continues to be transformed into economic activities that result in growth. Entrepreneurship itself is not an easy endeavour, it does not guarantee returns, and it very often results in failure (Geroski 1995). To help resolve this theoretical gap, the next section introduces the entrepreneurial filter theory, proposed in Prokop (2021). As the subsequent section shows, entrepreneurial filtration is a mechanism that processes knowledge into successful economic outcomes.

ENTREPRENEURIAL FILTER THEORY

Whilst the knowledge filter is considered a barrier to transforming knowledge into economic growth (Acs and Plummer 2005; Carlsson et al. 2007), the entrepreneurial filter explains the process of continuous transformation of knowledge and its further development (i.e. entrepreneurial venture) into economic growth. Whilst the knowledge filter, often portrayed as bureaucracy (Audretsch et al. 2006), is an obstacle solved by entrepreneurship, the entrepreneurial filter is a necessary catalyst at multiple stages of development of knowledge into a startup and startup into a successful company. As such, this section addresses the black box of knowledge conversion into economic growth, which remains obscured in the knowledge spillover theory of entrepreneurship. Essentially, it explains how newly generated knowledge becomes a successful company. In what follows, I draw the reader's attention to some of the key sources of technology entrepreneurship: the knowledge-generating universities, academic spinout companies, and university entrepreneurial ecosystems.

From Knowledge to Entrepreneurial Success

Knowledge produced at universities tends to be of uncertain character, given that it is rarely pursued for any application, but rather to advance our understanding of the world. This basic character makes it difficult to observe how university-generated knowledge can be turned into commercial application and subsequently economic growth. Yet such knowledge lends itself to entrepreneurship (Audretsch and Belitski 2021), as its uncertainty offers a greater economic reward to the entrepreneur, and subsequently to the economy (Vincett 2010). It is important to highlight that the pure stock of basic knowledge does not translate into innovation without any additional applied research and development activity (Henard and McFadyen 2005). Instead, it remains just 'shelved knowledge', often published but not commercialised. The American Bayh–Dole Act 1980 was a stimulant policy to improve this knowledge underutilisation problem and has sparked a substantial increase in university knowledge commercialisation activity (Carlsson et al. 2007). This successful policy has been replicated in other countries, like the UK, Germany, and Italy, to transfer the ownership of intellectual property to the university (Knie and Lengwiler 2008), with similar outcomes.

Whilst knowledge underutilisation has been addressed with this policy intervention, not all knowledge, not even all knowledge of commercial potential, becomes translated into spinout companies, and consequently economic growth. There are two key explanations for this problem: (a) scarcity of resources to devote to commercialisation activity; and (b) readiness of knowledge or its immediate applicability to the current technological paradigm of the markets.

The first is concerned with the economic reality in which knowledge is created and morphs into growth. With limited resources available, it remains difficult to support the economic exploitation of each piece of knowledge generated at universities, especially when some knowledge is more cost-effective to commercialise, whilst other knowledge despite not being cost-effective can lead to substantial economic growth outcomes. At the same time, the remaining knowledge may be less economically productive, i.e. the cost of commercialising it may be close to or outstrip the economic benefits it generates. I depict this problem in Figure 6.1.

Applied knowledge has already been created to solve practical problems. As such, its commercialisation costs are possibly the lowest, and much of the applied knowledge is expected to generate good economic returns. It is therefore related positively to entrepreneurial intentions of academics (Prodan and Drnovsek 2010). In comparison, *basic knowledge* is difficult to commercialise; it is more likely to lead to radical innovations and consequently to greater

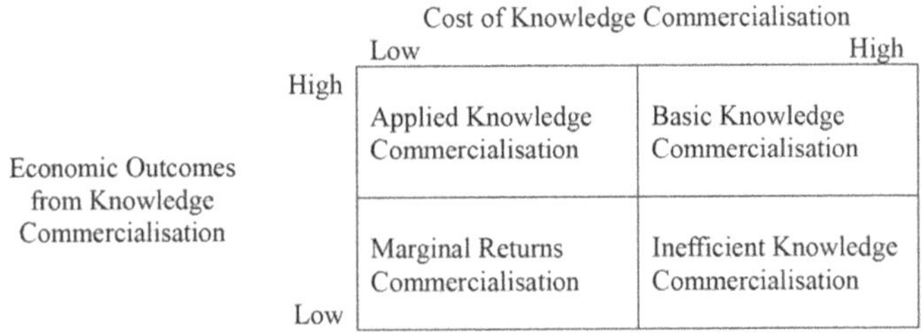

	Cost of Knowledge Commercialisation	
	Low	High
High Economic Outcomes from Knowledge Commercialisation **Low**	Applied Knowledge Commercialisation	Basic Knowledge Commercialisation
	Marginal Returns Commercialisation	Inefficient Knowledge Commercialisation

Figure 6.1   Knowledge commercialisation: costs and outcomes

economic outcomes (Vincett 2010). However, the complexity of commercialising it will bear a higher level of translational costs. *Marginal returns* are concerned with knowledge that may be of applied or basic character, but where commercialising it does not generate large economic returns (Harrison and Leitch 2010), even though the cost of doing so is quite low. This may be due to markets being very small/niche for the products and services so created. Whilst positive economic returns are observed, these may be outstripped by other forms of returns, e.g. social or environmental benefits. Lastly, the *inefficient knowledge commercialisation* quadrant is concerned with the stocks of knowledge where use is difficult to identify, and even if applied aspects exist, the cost of commercialisation is greater than any economic returns generated. This is not to say that such knowledge has no utility, it may just have benefits that are predominantly non-economic in character.

The second explanation for knowledge underutilisation lies in the fact that some knowledge may not be ready for the markets or markets may not be ready for the knowledge (Prokop 2017). This is more likely to be a problem for university-derived basic knowledge than for that generated through private sector research and development, which tends to solve immediate company problems. Knowledge that is not ready for commercialisation may require further development to identify its application potential. In this case, it may be too basic in its current form, but hold enough applied potential to be exploited within the technological paradigm of the markets. Conversely, some knowledge generated at universities may have no immediate application, as its basic nature may not reveal any immediate applications. Alternatively, it may solve consumer problems but to turn it into a product or service would result in something that is too advanced for the technological paradigm of the current markets, it may not fit or correspond with existing technologies, or it may require much of the current market technology to be upgraded to one that commercially does not exist yet. Such knowledge may become a latent entrepreneurial opportunity (Caiazza et al. 2020).

Given that finite resources do not allow the generation of greater levels of knowledge at universities, as national budgets tend to be spent on other priorities than academic research, the same problem concerns knowledge commercialisation. This includes resources necessary to determine the readiness of knowledge for commercialisation or resources needed to wait long enough for the markets to 'technologically' mature. With *Total Knowledge Generated* and the presence of the *Knowledge Filter*, the efficiency of employment of resources to commercialise knowledge is represented by parameter ε. As such *Commercialised Knowledge* is always lower than *Total Knowledge Generated*. Whilst barriers (i.e. the knowledge filter) have an exogeneous character, the ε

is endogenous in character, i.e. it is determined by the configuration of a university entrepreneurial ecosystem.

Commercialised Knowledge = Total Knowledge Generated
+ Knowledge Filter + ε   (6.1)

What is the *ε* parameter? The efficiency of knowledge conversion is dependent on the selectivity processes that start at the source of knowledge. At universities newly generated knowledge becomes a disclosure once some commercial opportunity/applicability for it has been determined. This is often performed not just by academics themselves, but often with involvement of technology transfer officers (Vohora et al. 2004). Such disclosure is still not a company. In fact, it remains a pre-company potential, as it enters its next stage of evaluation with prototype and market research, often key considerations for venture capitalists (Wright et al. 2006). Essentially, only commercial opportunities that work in principle and with a ready market for them should be commercialised, especially in bigger markets. Here, many opportunities are sifted, and the university supports the formation of spinout companies when this is commercially supported (Hayter 2013).

Whilst some universities try to attract investment at this stage many do so after the company is started. This investment attraction is really another selectivity phase, where typically early stage venture capitalists assess the future viability of spinout companies, before they commit financial resources to support their development (Vohora et al. 2004). There may be another stage where spinout companies join an incubator/accelerator programme, which typically assesses companies against its criteria prior to admission (Clarysse et al. 2005). The financing evaluation may take another number of rounds and include other sources of funding, e.g. banks or government grants. Furthermore, this evaluation also includes the market which is the most important actor in the multiple rounds of selectivity, as it determines whether the company will actually be successful by judging utility of its products or services built from the original university knowledge (Prokop 2021). Overall, what is important is that at each stage of knowledge development university entrepreneurial ecosystem actors participate in deciding about the efficient employment of ecosystemic resources to produce successful companies. These in turn may fuel the university entrepreneurial ecosystem with additional resources for the future. These rounds of selectivity that determine efficient use of resources to create successful companies are neatly portrayed as the *Entrepreneurial Filter* in Prokop (2021), which is the *ε* parameter. As such, equation (6.1) is revised as below:

Commercialised Knowledge = *Total Knowledge Generated*
+ *Knowledge Filter* + *Entrepreneurial Filter* (6.2)

I define the entrepreneurial filter (also alternatively referred to in this book as Prokop's filtration) as concerned with the commercial success of knowledge; it is manifested and performed by university entrepreneurial ecosystem actors that take part in evaluating commercial opportunities of knowledge at first, and companies later on, to ensure that at any moment in time the most applicable knowledge with the right human capital is exploiting it – leading to productive or economically efficient knowledge commercialisation. Consequently, some knowledge may not end up being commercially successful, which could be because it had insufficient scope, scale, or novelty level, or its exploitation was done poorly.

The entrepreneurial filter is essentially concerned with the efficiency or productivity of commercialisation and penetration of the knowledge filter. In a scenario where *Entrepreneurial Filter* = 0 in equation (6.2), knowledge of limited commercial or economic value may be consuming economic resources, cannibalising efforts to divert the same resources to more promising opportunities that can result in economic growth or greater economic growth. For some knowledge, it may be that it is too advanced for the current technological paradigm of the markets, in which case it may be commercialised later, as a latent entrepreneurial opportunity (Caiazza et al. 2020) – once the markets make the necessary technological leap. Entrepreneurial filter is critical to minimising such mismatch – as it is economically easier to adapt the technology to markets rather than markets to technologies. Figure 6.2 presents the entrepreneurial filter theory diagrammatically.

In short, every stage of entrepreneurial filtration results in a more refined population of successful academic spinout companies. It could be considered alternatively as a knowledge survival framework to express the journey that knowledge makes towards its growth contribution. As such, filtration purifies the population of companies – enabling only the most successful ones or companies of the highest economic potential to continue into the future. Each filtration stage determines the efficiency of resource allocation, with many companies finding themselves in the difficult position of non-allocation. This does not necessarily mean that such companies are failures. There are many reasons why passing through the entrepreneurial filter is impossible, and some of these could be related to the inability of the management team to convince the 'selection panel' – i.e. university entrepreneurial ecosystem actors, a round of bad decisions that could still be rectified but is viewed negatively by the 'selection panel', or wrong timing for the underlying technology in responding to current market needs. On the other hand, it could be that a filtration element

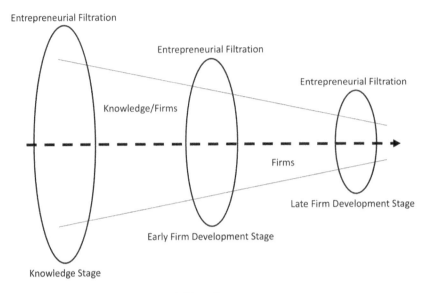

Figure 6.2   *Entrepreneurial filter theory*

is miscalibrated, resulting in finer filtration, wrong selection, or letting through too many companies with limited future potential.

How many rounds of entrepreneurial filtration lead to a successful company? The answer to this question would predominantly depend on how success is defined. Much of the entrepreneurial ecosystems literature is concerned with firm formation (e.g. Stam 2015; Ryan et al. 2021), which is an important aspect, but it does not itself guarantee economic growth unless these firms establish a presence in their markets. I try to model the *knowledge stage* filtration effect in the next chapter. One measure of success could follow firm survival (e.g. Prokop et al. 2019, 2024; Huggins et al. 2017), as it is not concerned with performance, but rather the ability to continue operations over a period of time. It has some obvious limitations – some companies may be surviving but not performing well, although eventually this may lead to failure.

Another good measure would be to observe a company reaching a particular stage of growth that corresponds to success (e.g. Vohora et al. 2004). This could be a form of an exit for investors, for example an initial public offering (Lawton Smith et al. 2008) or acquisition (Mason and Harrison 2006), positively related to survival (Prokop et al. 2019). Investment exits signify a successful development of a company, although in the case of academic spinouts, even at initial public offering stage, the companies may be generating no profits nor have a product to sell (Siegel et al. 2007). An alternative approach could be when companies reach a maturity and reorganisation stage, which on average concludes around 20 years of firm operations (Prokop and Kitagawa 2022). Whilst reaching this stage may appear like a long-term goal in terms of measurement of economic effects, Vincett (2010) suggests that the growth of academic spinouts levels off at around 30–35 years. For practical reasons, investment exit could be an elegant solution, even though its timing may vary across companies. Until this point, any company will have undergone multiple rounds of entrepreneurial filtration, confirming a pathway towards success.

Evidence from Prokop (2021) illustrates the functioning of the entrepreneurial filter for university knowledge and resultant academic spinouts. Additional evidence can be sought in the critical role of technology transfer offices (Shane 2004), venture capitalists (Wright et al. 2006; Prokop et al. 2019), etc. However, there has not been a more comprehensive empirical effort to establish the calibration of the entrepreneurial filter across a whole university entrepreneurial ecosystem. For example, in some university entrepreneurial ecosystems too many disclosures become translated into spinout companies, but not many of these companies remain successful (Prokop 2021). This suggests that the mere presence of ecosystemic elements that filter knowledge and its refined products (i.e. companies) (Prokop 2022) is not a guarantee of efficiency in resource allocation. Instead, the actual functioning needs better understanding to determine what makes each of the individual entrepreneurial filtration stages effective.

APPLYING THE CONCEPT TO GENERAL ECOSYSTEMS

Entrepreneurial filter theory (EFT) explains the mechanism of converting knowledge into entrepreneurial success, and consequently economic growth. It presents actors and elements of entrepreneurial ecosystems as performing a multi-stage filtering function to select knowledge of the highest commercial potential to become a successful company. Importantly, mere firm formation does not guarantee positive economic outcomes, what does is when these companies generate substantial economic outcomes that outpace the cost of generating them. In effect, EFT is concerned with the efficiency of converting knowledge into economic growth.

The filtration mechanism has been observed within the university entrepreneurial ecosystems, which uniquely enable the study of what happens to knowledge at the knowledge source. However, there is a broader appeal of the theory. Whilst place-based entrepreneurial ecosystems are preoccupied with high-growth entrepreneurship, little conceptual effort has gone into what various actors and elements of entrepreneurial ecosystems actually do to generate outputs that lead to economic growth outcomes.

This chapter attempted to explain this, by showing how the entrepreneurial ecosystem does not just create conditions for entrepreneurship, but it also performs entrepreneurial filtration, an important mechanism that resolves the problem of allocating scarce resources to support first knowledge and later companies with the highest probability of success. In essence, the entrepreneurial filtration theory explains the full journey of knowledge towards becoming part of economic growth. As such it builds on the knowledge spillover theory of entrepreneurship (Audretsch and Lehman 2005; Acs, Braunerhjelm, Audretsch and Carlsson 2009; Ghio et al. 2015; Shu et al. 2022), adding another layer of clarity to the processes that convert knowledge into economic growth, showing how the knowledge filter presents exogeneous obstacles, whilst the entrepreneurial filter represents an endogenous process of the 'purification' of knowledge into economic success.

Implications for Policy

The entrepreneurial filter theory explains the functioning of entrepreneurial ecosystems, but notably leaves policymakers with a difficult problem. Much of policymaking effort has been expended on supporting knowledge commercialisation and growing companies. Where EFT adds value is in pointing out that any policy aimed at entrepreneurship or the support of growing or innovating firms needs to be designed to function as a filtration mechanism. Whilst it is worthwhile to support more companies, policymakers are trusted with limited resources from taxpayers and need to utilise those to maximise taxpayers' value.

Whilst the EFT in this current form does not present a recipe of how to ensure optimal selectivity, it is upon policymakers to make regular assessments of how their support programmes perform in the long run – essentially building in a learning loop to calibrate its own filtration mechanism. What policymakers cannot do is to operate generic support programmes that support any knowledge or any company that signs up, essentially negating the existence of EFT.

Implications for Entrepreneurs

Forming a company and ensuring its success is a complex long-term process that requires the commitment of resources and good decision-making to secure business viability. Entrepreneurs, including academic, need to be aware that their entrepreneurial ecosystem offers support that is predicated on assessment of their past business experience and/or future plans. In essence, their performance is being evaluated to enable them to reach the next growth stage, a logic reflected in Vohora et al.'s (2004) model.

Whilst entrepreneurial filtration may be discouraging for some, knowing that there are criteria or a pathway forward offers a lot of optimism. As new cohorts of entrepreneurs learn from their entrepreneurial ecosystems what makes a successful venture, a better commercialisation process will establish itself – converting more knowledge into increasingly more successful ventures. With better calibrated entrepreneurial filters, ecosystems may accumulate more resources to support future waves of entrepreneurs (Mason and Harrison 2006). As such, positive long-term performance of entrepreneurial ecosystems is important to increasing a stock of successful enterprises, the ecosystem's effectiveness and capacity for support, leading to positive growth outcomes for the local/regional economy.

Implications for an Ecosystem's Actors

It is important that actors forming entrepreneurial ecosystems recognise that their role has a dual character: supportive and selective. This duality comes with great responsibility for overall ecosystem performance. In essence, actors taking part in the distribution of ecosystemic resources, be it coaching, mentoring, incubation, finance, advice, talent, or leadership, play a pivotal role in selecting the most commercially viable knowledge and sharpening its commercialisation outcomes into successful ventures. In essence, the role of such actors is in maximising the economic outcomes of knowledge generated within an ecosystem.

For emerging entrepreneurial ecosystems past history does not exist or may have too short a span to perform calibration of their entrepreneurial filter. With time each entrepreneurial ecosystem can develop a well-calibrated entrepreneurial filtration mechanism, where each actor reaches optimal performance within their unique institutional context. It is important to stress that in some entrepreneurial ecosystems actors may take longer to receive feedback and learn about the effectiveness of their filtration. Successful models of entrepreneurial ecosystems reveal well-calibrated entrepreneurial filtration, and have been observed in Silicon Valley (Saxenian 1994), or London's University Entrepreneurial Ecosystem (Prokop 2021). In extreme cases, actors may be encouraged to adopt ineffective practices, where the institutional or spatial setup prevents them from following a positive learning path, leading to support for a greater proportion of knowledge or companies that reveal low success probabilities.

CONCLUSION

The goal of this chapter was to explain the key mechanism in entrepreneurial ecosystems that explains the success of first knowledge and later companies.

Observing university entrepreneurial ecosystems enables more than just observation of sub-ecosystem dynamics. University entrepreneurial ecosystems are uniquely structured around the source of knowledge – in itself a source of entrepreneurship. Entrepreneurial filter theory builds on the knowledge spillover theory of entrepreneurship by revealing a mechanism that ensures effective allocation of resources to efficiently penetrate the knowledge filter and convert knowledge into economic growth. Actors of entrepreneurial ecosystems have very important economic roles. Whilst a composition of an entrepreneurial ecosystem is important to ensure presence of entrepreneurial filtration, its calibration is dependent on feedback and learning processes.

Entrepreneurial ecosystems operating successful entrepreneurial filtration increase their resources and stocks of successfully commercialised knowledge. As such, the quality of entrepreneurship rather than its quantity is important (Lafuente et al. 2023), but quantity of firms is expected to grow with improved calibration of entrepreneurial filtration.

7. Why some university entrepreneurial ecosystems perform better than others

Recognising entrepreneurial sub-ecosystems introduces an added layer of complexity to understanding place-based entrepreneurial ecosystems, in particular by observing how university entrepreneurial ecosystems are configured to operate individualistically, even when co-located and in theory having spatially proximate availability of actors and elements. The purpose of this chapter is to show why university entrepreneurial ecosystems perform differently with a focus on academic spinout company formation and survival. Importantly, university entrepreneurial ecosystems draw advantages from their composition and filtration mechanism, the configuration of which determines patterns of spinout activity.

PERFORMANCE OF UNIVERSITY ENTREPRENEURIAL ECOSYSTEMS

Studies of academic spinout companies typically point out a number of aspects that explain their formation. These predominantly include a university's knowledge generation efforts, often depicted as patents (Fini et al. 2011; Gonzalez-Pernia et al. 2013) or in pre-spinout ideas – i.e. disclosures (Di Gregorio and Shane 2003; Prokop and Thompson 2023). In other words, universities that do not generate much knowledge would struggle to have a portfolio of ideas that may have a commercial potential, as such research-intensive universities or those that are recognised for their quality/reputation have a higher predisposition towards forming greater numbers of spinout companies (Jensen et al. 2003). Examples of such universities include MIT (US), Stanford (US), Oxford (UK), Edinburgh (UK), ETH Zurich (Switzerland), KIT (Germany), and Ghent (Belgium). University entrepreneurial ecosystems that are built around such universities are expected to perform better than those that do not.

Patenting itself may also be important for spinout company success. For example, within certain sectors, such as biotechnology, it reassures the investors of the uniqueness of the underlying intellectual property and its ability to stave off competition owing to the monopoly nature of patents (Shane 2004). The intellectual property is most likely the only competitive resource of a newly formed spinout company (Prokop 2023), with its success dependent on it, for example in raising venture capital (Clarysse et al. 2007) to ensure company development. It has been found that nearly 70% of UK academic spinouts used patents to secure that competitive advantage (Hewitt-Dundas 2015).

However, much of the research on academic spinouts did not acknowledge the existence of university entrepreneurial ecosystems, resulting in comparisons of performance across universities with a focus on internal university characteristics (Clarysse, Wright and Van de Velde 2011; Bonardo et al. 2011; Åstebro et al. 2013; Gonzalez-Pernia et al. 2013) or spinout properties (Sciarelli et al. 2021) rather than the wider ecosystem that universities organise and co-ordinate. Whilst the literature has been partially recognising some external elements, e.g. networks with entrepreneurs, access to incubators (Bourelos et al. 2012; De Turi and Antonicelli 2019), local economic environment and institutions (Fini et al. 2017; Hossinger et al. 2020), such work provided only a partial account explaining academic spinout activity.

By recognising a wider framework of university entrepreneurial ecosystems it has been shown that university entrepreneurial ecosystems characterised by a greater completeness of ecosystem elements tend to generate larger numbers of academic spinouts (Prokop 2022). This is an important observation, as to understand why one university may be responsible for more academic spinouts it cannot be viewed merely through its internal resources and culture, but rather also through the external setup – its ecosystem. Early works that recognised the importance of university entrepreneurial ecosystems drew predominantly from network theory, which enabled connecting actors and elements (e.g. Hayter 2016; Hayter et al. 2018; Prokop et al. 2019). This is critical, as networks are an underlying structure of entrepreneurial ecosystems (Stam 2015) and have been recognised as essential in academic spinout studies (Vohora et al. 2004; Lawton Smith et al. 2008), yet rarely explored empirically (e.g. Rasmussen et al. 2015; Scholten et al. 2015; Prokop and Kitagawa 2022). It is only when following the connections that an image of an ecosystem may emerge.

Whilst spinout quantity has attracted many scholarly outputs, it is recognised that a looser early filtration mechanism (Prokop 2021) is what leads to greater formation of spinout companies. Conversely, the quality of academic spinouts requires a tighter filtration throughout their lifecycle. This is where university entrepreneurial ecosystems play important roles – recognising that the presence or absence of each ecosystemic actor/element may lend a hand or impose a barrier to their success. For example, university entrepreneurial ecosystems that have less experienced technology transfer offices or limited access to venture capital community may contribute to lower success rates of their spinouts (Prokop et al. 2019).

Recognising that studies drawing attention towards composition and filtration in university entrepreneurial ecosystems have not examined these characteristics on a wider sample and across both formation and survival metrics, it becomes critical to find out how these explain the performance of university entrepreneurial ecosystems. This is especially important given that university entrepreneurial ecosystems that focus on one type of metric – e.g. formation – may co-ordinate their configuration in a way that prevents their academic spinouts from better long-term success rates (Prokop 2021). In other words, policy prescriptions need to recognise that quantity and quality of academic spinouts generated from university entrepreneurial ecosystems may have different requirements (Fini et al. 2017). Therefore, understanding how the success of academic spinouts is dependent on a university entrepreneurial ecosystem's characteristics poses a challenge, especially in advising policymakers interested in supporting this activity as part of a wider industrial or innovation-leaning policy.

The purpose of this chapter is to empirically investigate what explains performance differences between university entrepreneurial ecosystems, with a particular interest in their co-located character, filtration, and composition or completeness. The following section outlines the empirical approach.

METHODOLOGY

To achieve data consistency I use the sample employed in Chapter 3, this time with a different focus. First, co-located university entrepreneurial ecosystems are identified based on their presence in the same city/town or not. There are two exceptions owing to complicated administrative geography of UK cities: London and Manchester. London is composed of multiple local authorities and a single upper-tier governing body (Slack and Côté 2014); as such it is classified here at a city-region level to capture this complicated urban governance structure or spatial coverage. Conversely, Manchester has two contiguous local authorities: Salford and Trafford, which are included together under a single place-based entrepreneurial ecosystem to represent university entrepreneurial ecosystems within it (they are spatially proximate and operating in what constitutes a single urban area, but administratively and historically belonging to three different local authorities). There are 11 cities that contain 33 co-located university entrepreneurial ecosystems (with London hosting 11). Whilst there may be more co-located university entrepreneurial ecosystems, I employ a very specific sample, which excludes many universities and their ecosystems (for the keen reader I recommend revisiting Chapter 3 for the methodological note).

The analysis has a two-fold approach. First, it examines the co-location character by looking at differences across a number of variables that define spinout activity. I look at the rate of variation within co-located university entrepreneurial ecosystems as per their respective place-based entrepreneurial ecosystem, and test whether university entrepreneurial ecosystems differ owing to co-location or non-co-location character. To do this, I employ a Mann–Whitney *U*-test to account for the non-parametric nature of the data.

Second, I explain the performance of university entrepreneurial ecosystems by observing their outcomes in terms of spinout formation and survival. I fit a negative binomial regression model to account for overdispersion of the dependent variables. The dependent variables are obtained from HEBCIS and represent the number of spinout companies formed between 2014/15 and 2020/21 (*Spinouts formed*), and the number of spinout companies that survived for at least 3 years captured in 2020/21 (*3-year survival*). The modelling includes three independent variables: *UEE composition*, *Co-location*, and *Filtration*. The first represents the number of elements a university entrepreneurial ecosystem is made of, with a minimum of two and maximum of seven (with Chapter 3 offering a detailed explanation of these elements). The second is a dummy which checks whether a university entrepreneurial ecosystem has a co-located character, whilst the last employs Prokop's (2021) filtration, with a caveat that it merely captures the early *knowledge stage* (i.e. how many spinouts emerge from disclosures). I control for three aspects: number of *Disclosures* generated (across 2014/15–2020/21), *GDP per capita* (gross domestic product) recorded for 2014 and accounting for spatial complexities explained above, and *Past survival performance* for the survival model only. This includes survival rates of spinout companies calculated for each university entrepreneurial ecosystem from firms formed between 1959 and 2013 with their status checked in 2014, as captured from data used in Prokop et al. (2019).

The descriptive statistics as well as correlations are presented in Table 7.1. Whilst there are a number of statistically significant correlations among the independent variables and controls, these are weak to moderate in strength.

There are no multicollinearity issues in the models with variance inflation factors recorded remaining at a level of 1.5 or below for both models and all variables, well below the conventional thresholds that may indicate any cause for concern. I also tested an ordinary least squares (OLS) specification for robustness with log-transformation applied to the dependent variables, to ensure that the results stay stable even if a modelling approach changes.

FINDINGS

In order to assess the co-located character of university entrepreneurial ecosystems and how it relates to their performance, I look at the level of variation (or range across variables) within a co-located sub-sample, non-co-located

Table 7.1   Descriptive statistics and correlations

Variables	Mean	Standard deviation	N	1	2	3	4	5	6	7
1 Spinouts formed	11.67	19.51	60	1						
2 3-year survival	13.07	22.16	60	0.937**	1					
3 UEE composition	5.82	1.28	60	0.259*	0.262*	1				
4 Co-location	0.55	0.50	60	0.208	0.125	-0.289*	1			
5 Filtration	0.06	0.11	60	-0.048	-0.113	-0.326*	0.104	1		
6 Disclosures	369.28	515.61	60	0.868**	0.855**	0.285*	0.245	-0.212	1	
7 GDP per capita	38,694.84	13,276.55	60	0.244	0.230	-0.342**	0.483**	0.250	0.190	1
8 Past survival performance	0.77	0.28	56	0.086	0.115	-0.268*	0.055	-0.004	0.112	-0.028

Note: * Statistically significant at a 5% level; ** statistically significant at a 1% level.

sub-sample and a full sample. For the co-located sub-sample, I also inspect the extremes in its variation. This approach allows the data to be disentangled, by showing the reality of co-located university entrepreneurial ecosystems *vis-à-vis* non-co-located ones, as presented in Table 7.2.

The average difference in a co-located sub-sample is estimated by finding an arithmetic mean from the maximum variation at each place-based entrepreneurial ecosystem. It shows that co-located university entrepreneurial ecosystems vary in their configurations, function, and performance. Some co-located university entrepreneurial ecosystems have extreme variations at a place-based entrepreneurial ecosystem level, with the highest difference for numbers of spinouts formed coming at 117, nearly no different than a similar extreme observed in a full sample (of 118). A similar story is observed among the spinouts that survived for at least 3 years (116 vs. 117), completeness of the university entrepreneurial ecosystem (five elements), or filtration (0.67). This suggests that co-located university entrepreneurial ecosystems may not enjoy benefits of co-location, when parallel benefits tend to be enjoyed by clustered businesses. In fact, this indicates a relatively separate, individualistic, or isolationist character that universities, as key organising actors, maintain. Whilst some of the co-located university entrepreneurial ecosystems report lower variation – e.g. in Leicester or Liverpool, these represent a minority of cases, and merely across a limited number of measures. A key explanation for such variations can be found in the knowledge generation ability of co-located universities, where typically in each such location there will be at least one research-intensive university and at least one teaching-oriented one. On average cities with co-located university entrepreneurial ecosystems are larger (in terms of population) and characterised by higher levels of economic development (as measured by GDP per capita), both statistically significant results. These parameters make it even more perplexing that university entrepreneurial ecosystems show limited evidence of benefits of co-location.

Interestingly, across the measures observed here the variations in a non-co-located sub-sample are lower than the highest differences observed in a co-located sub-sample, further adding to evidence that co-location may offer no advantage to university entrepreneurial ecosystems. As such, university entrepreneurial ecosystems may pose a challenge for local policymakers in that their non-cooperative nature may be detrimental to place-based entrepreneurial ecosystems' overall outcomes, given that connectivity across entrepreneurial ecosystems or sub-ecosystems leads to positive entrepreneurial outputs (Prokop and Thompson 2023).

When the co-located sub-sample is compared with the non-co-located sub-sample, no discernible differences are found across most measures describing university entrepreneurial ecosystems with the exception of their completeness. Whilst a statistically significant difference is observed, the

Table 7.2   *The characteristics of co-located university entrepreneurial ecosystems*

		UEE completeness 2015/16	Prokop's (2021) filtration between 2014/15 and 2020/21	Number of spinouts formed between 2014/15 and 2020/21	Active spinouts that survived at least 3 years	GDP per capita 2021
Co-located UEEs	Average differences	1.91	0.09	29.55	29.82	NR
	Highest difference	5.00	0.67	117.00	116.00	NR
	Lowest difference	0.00	0.00	4.00	1.00	NR
Non-co-located UEEs	Difference	4.00	0.25	58.00	107.00	NR
All UEEs	Difference	5.00	0.67	118.00	117.00	NR
Co-located vs. non-co-located UEEs	*U*-test	**	NS	NS	NS	***

Note: NR, not reported – measuring differences in PBEE's GDP for co-located UEEs results in 0; NS, not statistically significant; ** statistically significant at a 5% level; *** statistically significant at a 1% level.

finding adds to the picture painted with the data thus far – meaning that on average co-located university entrepreneurial ecosystems show lower levels of completeness than their non-co-located counterparts. In other words, co-location (or proximity) is not related to shared access to ecosystemic actors/ elements and shared resources, which could be the main benefit of co-location, alluded to in Degroof and Roberts (2004), who suggested that universities should co-operate more to strengthen their commercialisation efforts.

The conclusion that can be drawn so far shows that co-location offers no or at least very limited benefits to university entrepreneurial ecosystems. Instead it uncovers disconnected and independent character of university entrepreneurial ecosystems.

To inspect the performance of university entrepreneurial ecosystems, I run simple regression models fitting the university entrepreneurial characteristics: *Composition*, *Co-location*, and *Filtration*, and controlling for levels of knowledge generation, past performance, and local economic conditions. The results, including the ordinary least squares robustness tests, confirm the observation made above, as presented in Table 7.3. Co-location is not related to the performance of university entrepreneurial ecosystems, whether this is measured by the numbers of companies formed or their survival. This distilled result shows how university entrepreneurial ecosystems lead largely independent operations, where counterintuitively proximity does not induce entrepreneurial performance benefits.

However, two characteristics of university entrepreneurial ecosystems reveal how these differ in performance. First, pertaining to the structure of university entrepreneurial ecosystems, their composition (or completeness) shows a positive and statistically significant coefficient across both formation and survival measures. What this means is that university entrepreneurial ecosystems that are more complete, or with a greater number of constituent actors/elements, are associated with larger numbers of spinout companies formed and their survival. Conversely, university entrepreneurial ecosystems that are less developed in terms of their composition would show lower levels of performance. This is an interesting finding, confirming the importance of composition (Prokop 2022) and not just specific actors/elements (e.g. Fini et al. 2011, 2017; Prokop et al 2019).

Second, the functioning of university entrepreneurial ecosystems in terms of translating disclosures into spinout numbers indicates that university entrepreneurial ecosystems with looser entrepreneurial filters are related to more spinout companies, confirming Prokop's (2021) work. In other words, the less selective a university entrepreneurial ecosystem is with its disclosures or generated knowledge of commercial potential, the higher the chance of generating more spinout companies. This is an unsurprising effect. However, no such relationship is found with a survival measure, suggesting that entrepreneurial

Table 7.3   *Regression results of spinouts formed and 3-year survival*

	NB		OLS	
	Spinouts formed	3-year survival	Spinouts formed (log)	3-year survival (log)
UEE composition	0.328 (0.135)**	0.267 (0.158)*	0.273 (0.111)**	0.231 (0.127)*
Co-location	0.080 (0.236)	−0.049 (0.237)	0.014 (0.220)	0.035 (0.228)
Filtration	0.288 (0.135)**	−0.092 (0.176)	0.250 (0.101)**	−0.057 (0.122)
Disclosures	0.819 (0.139)***	0.820 (0.151)***	0.787 (0.108)***	0.751 (0.114)***
GDP per capita	0.088 (0.128)	0.119 (0.134)	0.068 (0.113)	0.103 (0.121)
Past survival performance		0.266 (0.147)*		0.208 (0.106)*
Constant	1.896 (0.166)***	2.041 (0.169)***	1.865 (0.152)***	1.915 (0.158)***
Akaike information criterion	365.749	359.275		
Alpha	0.453 (0.114)	0.488 (0.117)		
R^2			0.627	0.639
N	60	56	60	56

Note: * Statistically significant at a 10% level; ** statistically significant at a 5% level; *** statistically significant at a 1% level.

filtration is not related to survival. In fact, the measure reports a negative coefficient here, even though it is statistically insignificant. Importantly, there are two explanations of this effect.

The filtration measure captured only an early stage, i.e. the *knowledge stage*, when entrepreneurial filtration takes place at each stage of company development, including post-formation. Prokop et al.'s (2019) study showed that actors that engage with academic spinout companies at later stages, such as venture capitalists, are found to be good predictors of survival – suggesting the later-stage entrepreneurial filtration mechanism. Alternatively, it may be that other factors than filtration are important to academic spinouts' survival as captured by the error term.

The control variables suggest that generating knowledge of commercial potential is one of the key characteristics of well-performing university entrepreneurial ecosystems. Interestingly, the level of economic development of a locality occupied by a university entrepreneurial ecosystem is unrelated to its spinout activity, suggesting that their performance does not rely on beneficial economic conditions. Therefore, university entrepreneurial ecosystems may have a transformative potential for their localities, as their performance is not related to levels of GDP per capita. However, other local conditions may be important, for example sectoral specialisation (Prokop et al. 2019) or the nature of the urban area (Van Geenhuizen and Soetanto 2013). It is unsurprising that past performance is a good predictor of future performance, confirming the importance of histories of entrepreneurship to the ecosystem's outcomes (Spigel 2017), enabling learning from past successes and offering a recycling of actors (Spigel and Vinodrai 2021; Walsh et al. 2023).

Limitations

The findings reported here are not without limitations. First, it is important to state that HEBCIS data do not allow the identification of a real survival rate, as they do not follow each specific company, but merely record aggregated data at university level. This crucially limits the potential to match company records and investigate more intricate company-level mechanisms. They also do not allow capturing of the specific duration of survival; instead merely a confirmed 3-year survival rate was modelled.

Second, the sample used here, whilst consistent, is not large – and a greater sample, ideally including cross-country data, could offer more insightful and precise estimation results.

Finally, the modelling does not test all possible characteristics of university entrepreneurial ecosystems, including the institutional aspects which may have a bearing on their performance (e.g. Fini et al. 2017). However, it is important to note that the results presented here show a need for further study, especially exploring the variable compositions (e.g. How many actors/elements is the maximum?) and operation of entrepreneurial filtration mechanism (e.g. Which actors take part in filtration at each stage? Is filtration a locally or spatially distributed activity?).

UNIVERSITY ENTREPRENEURIAL ECOSYSTEM PERFORMANCE MODEL

Performance of university entrepreneurial ecosystems is clearly different both at the level of measures used to evaluate it and across their functional and structural characteristics. The findings presented above indicate that university entrepreneurial ecosystems characterised by composition lacking multiple elements tend to generate less spinout companies and enjoy poorer survival outcomes. At the same time, the looser filtration mechanism of university entrepreneurial ecosystems is associated with higher numbers of spinout companies, but not survival. In fact, survival may be dependent on later stage and tighter filtration (Prokop 2021). These two features of university entrepreneurial ecosystems determine the quantity and quality of spinout companies, as highlighted in Figure 7.1. It is important to note that performance is also reliant on the munificence of resources available to university entrepreneurial ecosystems, their past histories, and accumulated experience.

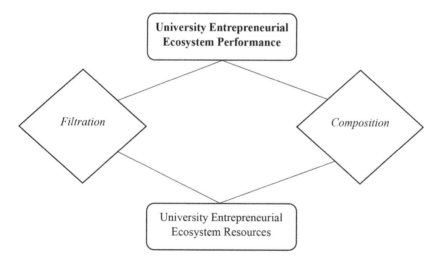

Figure 7.1   *Performance framework of university entrepreneurial ecosystems*

The findings presented here are critical to policymakers and university administrators that show interest in promoting such high technology venture creation by utilising the vast wealth of knowledge generated by universities. Essentially, the performance of university entrepreneurial ecosystems is not a simple outcome, and both short- and long-term goals and the quantity and quality of academic spinouts require careful calibration of the structure and function of university entrepreneurial ecosystems to avoid forming multiple companies destined for failure, or an insufficient number of firms to support local or regional economic development. For scholars interested in advising on the future direction of such policies the fundamental question lies in finding an optimum calibration of a university entrepreneurial ecosystem.

CONCLUSION

The variation in performance reveals a complex configuration of function and structure of university entrepreneurial ecosystems. Creating more spinout companies requires a different calibration than ensuring their post-formation development. In essence, the configuration of university entrepreneurial ecosystems needs to be responsive to the demands of the local portfolio of academic spinout companies at their different stages of development. Given the evolving model of university entrepreneurial ecosystems (Chapter 4), it is clear that the availability of actors is important, but their functionality needs to be carefully adjusted to cater to spinouts' evolving needs given local conditions (Sternberg 2014).

Successful university entrepreneurial ecosystems will reveal a unique ability to find a delicate balance in orchestrating their resources and networks to ensure performance expressed in venture numbers and their success. Such fine-tuned university entrepreneurial ecosystems will be well placed to contribute positively to local/regional economic development with successful high-technology companies creating employment opportunities for highly skilled individuals and attracting capital to local areas, potentially offering a contribution to peripheral places that goes beyond the formation of territorial knowledge pools (Benneworth and Charles 2005). Bolstering the performance of university entrepreneurial ecosystems by adjusting filtration and composition levels may be an attractive route for policymakers to enhance the economic futures of their areas.

8. Relocation of academic spinouts: 'leaky localism' of university entrepreneurial ecosystems

The location of academic spinout companies carries a lot of theoretical meaning, given that ecosystems are locally specific unique constructs that are influenced by their levels of available human capital, cultural and institutional setup, and underlying network structure (Stam 2015; Stam and Van de Ven 2021; Prokop and Thompson 2023). This chapter takes a look at spinout location. It is widely accepted in the academic spinout literature that these firms are born at departments and subsequently remain in the vicinity of their parent universities (Heblich and Slavtchev 2014). This is often explained by the requirement for strong knowledge links and the fact that academic founders typically continue their university employment. From the knowledge spillover theory of entrepreneurship we learn that knowledge spillovers tend to have a localised character (Audretsch and Lehmann 2005). However, early evidence from UK and US on academic spinouts suggests that not all of them remain in spatial proximity to parent universities (Lawton Smith et al. 2014; Avnimelech and Feldman 2015). Given the lack of comprehensive evidence, the focus of this chapter is to show what this phenomenon looks like within the case of UK, which may be informative for other national contexts. The chapter concludes by reflecting on the implications of academic spinout relocation on regional economic development.

WHY FIRMS RELOCATE?

Whilst firms become established in particular places, many of them do not continue their operations at their birth location. Firm relocation literature explains this through two key strands of studies: partial and full relocation (Brouwer et al. 2004; Carrincazeaux and Coris 2015). The first strand studies firms establishing new operations or moving part of their operations to another location. This may be related to growth, such as accessing new markets, whether domestic in another location or international (Brouwer et al. 2004; Kapitsinis 2017). At the same time, such a decision may also stem from the need to reassess the firm's cost base to identify a cheaper location, domestic or international (Wang et al. 2020). The second strand deals with firms moving all of their operations to another location, whilst closing all activities in current location. This may be related to firm growth, but such decision may also be dictated by the assessment of locational conditions (Vand Dijk and Pellenbarg 2000). The empirical focus of this chapter is on the complete move rather than merely a branch of operations.

The economic geography literature interested in relocation behaviour of firms has shown that the first key trigger for a firm to move office is its growth (Van Dijk and Pellenbarg 2000; Pellenbarg et al. 2002; Brouwer et al. 2004; Mariotti 2005; Weterings and Knoben 2013). Expansion of workforce means that requirements for premises change; this may be related to hosting more staff, but also more equipment or more sophisticated machinery. This trigger is typically unrelated to the assessment of spatial conditions, bar market demand; instead the relocation decision is a response to positive performance of a firm. In such cases, the relocating firms are more likely to find their next premises within the proximity of the original ones (Weterings and Knoben 2013), remaining within their place-based entrepreneurial ecosystems. In fact, for relocating startups, short distance relocations (e.g. within a region) are more likely to be followed by positive performance outcomes compared with longer distance moves, e.g. to another region (Lee 2022). As such growing new firms represent a positive economic output capture for local areas, and fall well within the discussions on the development of entrepreneurial ecosystems (Mack and Mayer 2016; Brown and Mason 2017; Nordling 2019), where firms stay, recycle and generally contribute to their ecosystems.

Another key trigger discussed in the literature is related to the costs of labour (Pellenbarg et al. 2002). The notion behind this is that firms make rational assessments of their locational situations, and when they identify a change in such locational conditions affecting their competitiveness – i.e. increasing labour costs – they may decide to find a location with cheaper input costs. However, it is important to highlight that before the 1990s economic policy directed at convergence of peripheral regions was predominantly based around labour costs as an attractive factor to lure firms away from richer core regions, but not afterwards (Mariotti 2005), as this may only be a factor for labour-intensive firms (Pennings and Sleuwaegen 2000). In fact, labour-intensive firms were found to be more likely to relocate than invest to upgrade their technologies to improve their competitiveness, as observed in a study of Chinese light manufacturing firms (Wang et al. 2020). Consequently, this may not be part of a very successful economic policy aimed at attracting firms to regions with low labour costs, as it does not attract productive firms to the peripheral regions. Instead, it leads to a spatial sorting effect, where low-productivity firms migrate towards economically peripheral regions, and high-productivity firms towards economically successful or core regions (Baldwin and Okubo 2006). Whilst this trigger is important, its importance to technology startups may be very limited.

Innovation, or lack of it, is another important trigger for firm relocation (Naz et al. 2015). Kreutzer and Mitze (2017) find that German firms engaging in product innovation are more likely to relocate domestically, observing that international relocations tend to be related to low innovation activity. Furthermore, innovative firms tend to relocate to regions characterised by higher levels of research and development activity and good quality of human capital (Naz et al. 2015), suggesting a spatial sorting effect again, where well-performing regions tend to perform well owing to the type of firms based in and attracted to such locations. This is a key factor explaining why innovative firms tend to be located in urban regions (Niebuhr et al. 2020). It is important to observe that a firm's innovative output is dependent on its employees, and as such any relocation decision needs to take into account changes in the commuting distance, as relocations that result in an increased commute lead to lower innovation output of employees (Xiao et al. 2021).

Another important trigger is the availability of financial capital to build a company (De Prijcker et al. 2019). Entrepreneurs have a limited ability to choose where they are originally located; as such, many firms may be registered in areas that lack necessary locational conditions to develop companies. For such firms relocation to access financial capital essential to development and growth may be critical. It is unsurprising to find studies highlighting access to finance as one of the key triggers of relocation (Kapitisinis 2017). Firms that make such moves tend to be more likely to actually attract venture finance (De Prijcker et al. 2019), indicating a strong localised effect of such capital. In the UK much of this capital is concentrated in London, leaving firms located elsewhere at a disadvantage in their growth efforts (Huggins and Prokop 2014).

Whilst the literature tries to classify these triggers into push and pull factors (Pellenbarg et al. 2002; Brouwer et al. 2004; Kronenberg 2013), as highlighted above, there is no clear delineation whether a particular factor is only push or pull in nature. What emerges instead is a picture of complexity of relocation activity, where each factor may both push a firm to move and at the same time pull it to a particular location.

Importantly, Yi (2018) expands this typology and draws attention to retention factors. This is theoretically critical, as firms also have to address the issues that discourage them from relocation. For example, spatial sorting suggests that firms that are innovative and born into urban regions of high levels of research and development activity would have a lower proclivity to relocate (Niebuhr et al. 2020), as they are already in the best possible place for them. Importantly, the sole cost of relocation may prove to be a retention factor, even though there may be strong push and pull factors. Firms that intend to relocate need to evaluate whether the cost of the move is below the level of benefits stemming from relocation (Van Dijk and Pellenbarg 2000; Pellenbarg et al. 2002; Lee 2022). Even though there may be clear benefits in doing business elsewhere, the relocation itself proves to be far from a frictionless activity. Consequently, it is important to stress that not all relocations, even though they may result from rational decision-making, lead to improved post-move performance (Gregory et al. 2005; Knoben and Oerlemans 2005; Lee 2022), with firms also severing their local networks (Atakhan-Kenneweg et al. 2021), pointing to a complex and risky nature of this activity.

THE SPATIALITY OF ACADEMIC SPINOUTS

Given the unique nature of academic spinout companies, their relocation patterns may be more complex than those of other firms. First, academic spinouts tend to be incubated at universities (within departments) (Hewitt-Dundas 2015; Prokop 2021); as such there is an expectation that their location will change as they develop, since universities, bar their incubators and science parks, do not offer commercial business space on continuous basis.

Second, academic spinouts are more likely to be in receipt of venture capital funding (Ortín-Ángel and Vendrell-Herrero 2010) and are characterised by high survival rates (Prokop et al. 2019), making their relocation decision more likely. Given their need for capital investment to develop business, the relocation may be related to spatial concentration of venture finance, which is especially more prevalent for firms that find themselves in regions with lower availability of venture capital (De Prijcker et al. 2019). For example, in the UK the key concentration is in London (Klagge and Martin 2005; Huggins and Prokop 2014), suggesting that UK academic spinouts are more likely to migrate there. Academic spinouts' longer survival indicates potential for a growth-related proximity move (Weterings and Knoben 2013), or in case growth is not realised – their move may result from the finite limits of university space or relocation for other reasons (Lawton Smith et al. 2014).

Third, academic spinouts require high quality human capital to sustain their innovation activity, and as such they are more likely to stay proximate to their parent university entrepreneurial ecosystem or, at the very least, within an urban area, given the spatial sorting effect (Niebuhr et al. 2020). This is important, as university researchers tend to be an important source of academic spinout staff (Boh et al. 2016), often having performed research together with academic founders, making them uniquely specialised and fit for technology development. Relatedly, the academic founder's lab or department where much of the underlying intellectual property was generated may have the right tools, equipment, technicians, or managerial support that are essential for technology development, inducing spatial retention (Yi 2018) of academic spinouts, as access to similar inputs elsewhere may be limited, prohibitively costly, or non-existent.

Fourth, on a pragmatic level, academic spinout founders tend to retain their university employments (Fini et al. 2009); as such their preference should be to stay spatially close to the parent university entrepreneurial ecosystem. This hassle factor is comparable with the cost of relocation (e.g. Pellenbarg et al. 2002), where it induces additional friction preventing academic spinouts from realising the extent of benefits offered by any new location. This suggests that there should be a limited relocation activity of academic spinouts, but evidence found by Avnimelech and Feldman (2015) in their study of US academic spinouts paints a more complex picture, with many of these firms found to be located further away from their parent university entrepreneurial ecosystems.

The range of hypothesised relocation behaviours of academic spinout companies indicates a clear gap in understanding what actually happens to them post-formation. In what follows, I attempt to depict the situation in the UK based on a robust sample of academic spinouts. Whilst the approach employed is descriptive, its purpose is to reveal the behaviour and trends in relocation patterns of academic spinouts. As such, I focus on the typical to relocation literature split between core and peripheral regions (Pellengbarg et al. 2002; Mariotti 2005; Baldwin and Okubo 2006; Weterings and Knoben 2013; Forslid and Okubo 2014; Gaubert 2018; Rossi and Dej 2020), which carries a lot of theoretical weight in explaining relocation patterns.

METHODOLOGY

In order to show a comprehensive picture of academic spinout relocations I employ data used in Prokop and Kitagawa (2022). The dataset covers 1331 academic spinout companies across 12 unitary regions of the UK. Each spinout's location represents a registered office address. To improve tracking relocations, I focus on 1200 single-parent spinouts of which 262 relocated. The reason behind this sample selection is to avoid counting relocations of spinouts that have multiple parents, where relocations may simply mean jumping from one parent's university entrepreneurial ecosystem location to another. Of 1200 academic spinouts 925 survived until 2014. Within the survivors 210 firms relocated, whilst 715 did not.

The relocation here is regarded as movement away from the university's unitary region. As a result, the migration among 715 spinouts may have happened, but at an intra-regional level. The concern for this chapter is an inter-regional relocation, which as outlined in previous sections is more difficult and less expected than intra-regional relocation.

FINDINGS

UK academic spinouts present an interesting case of relocation, given their unique nature as firms. It is important to stress that the direction of their relocations, as depicted in Figure 8.1, shows a high variety of moves that concern all UK unitary regions. Each of these regions is both in receipt and at loss of academic spinouts, indicating a wide spread of networks consequently developed.

Just over a fifth of UK academic spinouts relocated inter-regionally, as presented in Table 8.1. The key regions that observed the highest outflows of academic spinouts as a proportion of all those established within their university entrepreneurial ecosystems are: London (39%), the South West (33%), and the West Midlands (33%). Interestingly, the lowest outflows of academic spinouts were experienced by two of the three devolved nations of the UK: Northern Ireland (4%) and Scotland (5%), with Wales' (18%) outflows being in line with those of English regions such as the North West (17%) and the East Midlands (18%). These findings suggest that the most geographically remote regions (Northern Ireland and Scotland) have a higher retention rate of academic spinouts, signifying either good local university entrepreneurial ecosystem conditions or high costs of relocation deterring inter-regional migration.

The highest net recipients of academic spinouts were the South East (37 firms), the North West (10 firms), and London (9 firms) regions. London is particularly unique here, given that it also experiences the highest outflow of academic spinouts, potentially related to negative externalities of its high level of urbanisation (Lawton Smith et al. 2014), such as congestion or property prices. Conversely, the regions that experienced negative net flows, i.e. losing more spinout companies than they gain, are the West Midlands (15 firms), the North East (11 firms), and Yorkshire and the Humber (11 firms). Such high pressure to relocate may indicate push factors of these regions characterised by peripheral lock-in of their networks (Prokop and Kitagawa 2022), where academic spinouts struggle to access important actors from their parent university entrepreneurial ecosystems or other intra-regional ecosystems.

Academic spinouts are substantially attracted towards core regions of the UK as presented in Table 8.2, with 66% of academic spinouts having migrated towards them. Core regions include London, the South East and the East of England. This not surprising, given the spatial sorting effect predicting productive or innovative firms being drawn towards more productive regions (Baldwin and Okubo 2006). More than half of this relocation activity originates in other core regions of the UK. What remains theoretically interesting are the moves of academic spinouts to peripheral regions accounting for 34% of relocation activity. Relocations from core regions to peripheral regions constitute 13% of all relocations of academic spinouts, whilst those that

Note: Nodes depict unitary regions of the UK: nine English regions and the three devolved nations of Northern Ireland, Scotland, and Wales. The arrows depict the direction of relocation.

Figure 8.1   *Regional relocation patters of academic spinouts in the UK*

Table 8.1   Single-parent spinouts and relocation by region

	Number of spinouts formed in the region	Percentage outflow	Net flow
East Midlands	60	18.33	−1
East of England	89	29.21	1
London	160	39.38	9
North East	67	22.39	−11
Northern Ireland	56	3.57	−2
North West	87	17.24	10
Scotland	258	5.04	−8
South East	135	27.41	37
South West	63	33.33	−10
Wales	44	18.18	1
West Midlands	86	32.56	−15
Yorkshire and The Humber	95	24.21	−11
Total	1200	21.83	

Table 8.2   Spinout relocation by type of region (single parent spinouts)

	To core (%)	To periphery (%)
From core	35.50	12.60
From periphery	30.53	21.37

move from one peripheral region to another represent 21% of all relocations. Although these may be moves towards regions offering better conditions than where academic spinouts were born (especially among peripheral regions), the finding may also represent a different set of explanations, for example personal reasons or accessing peripherally located venture finance.

Figure 8.2 explores one of the key reasons startup companies, especially technology ones, relocate – i.e. access to finance (De Prijcker et al. 2019), which in the UK is more prevalent in the core regions (Huggins and Prokop 2014). For academic spinouts that did not take part in inter-regional reloca-tion, a greater proportion of those that stayed in core regions were in receipt of venture capital than those that remained in the peripheries, a statistically significant result.

A similar scenario is observed among academic spinouts that relocated to another region. A larger proportion of those that left core regions were in

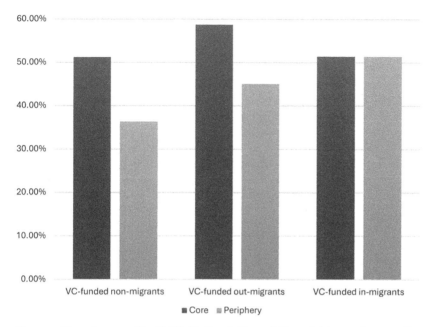

Note: Non-migrants – $U = 43{,}979.50$, $Z = -3.64$, $p < 0.01$, $r = 0.14$; out-migrants – $U =$ 4733.50, $Z = -1.97$, $p = 0.05$, $r = 0.14$.

Figure 8.2   *Percentage of venture capital-funded live spinouts by type of region and relocation (single-parent spinouts)*

receipt of venture capital compared with those that left peripheral regions, also a statistically significant result. Whilst the first finding was expected, given previous studies, the outmigration is an interesting result. It could be related to sourcing finance outside of spinouts' own core regions (maintaining the argument of relocating towards venture capital) or it could reveal a different motivation altogether.

Finally, when the destination of relocation is considered, there is no difference observed in venture capital funding for spinouts relocating to core or peripheral regions. This is peculiar, but it may suggest that both cohorts of firms realised their goals for relocation, such as the aforementioned access to capital.

'LEAKY LOCALISM' AND ITS IMPLICATIONS FOR REGIONAL ECONOMIC DEVELOPMENT

University entrepreneurial ecosystems clearly do not exist as self-contained units typically depicted in entrepreneurial ecosystems literature. They build wider networks to connect with actors outside of their locale (Prokop 2021) and connect with other university entrepreneurial ecosystems (Prokop and Thompson 2023). Whilst these insights may have assumed that university entrepreneurial ecosystems have a unique spatial design, there is a more intricate picture painted by the findings presented in this chapter. The outputs of university entrepreneurial ecosystems – academic spinout companies – are migratory firms, they relocate away from parent university entrepreneurial ecosystems. This migration is not a special rare event; instead it underpins the unique nature of academic spinout companies. As they grow, academic spinouts reassess their needs and decide on a location that may be more beneficial to their business (Pellenbarg et al. 2002). This finding is critical and builds on works of Lawton Smith et al. (2014) and Avnimelech and Feldman (2015), and contributes to the theorisations of academic spinout companies (Prokop 2023), outlining the scope of relocation activity of academic spinout companies.

For university entrepreneurial ecosystems it adds another flavour of complexity, where their localised character is no longer dominant. Instead, this chapter has shown that the localism of university entrepreneurial ecosystems is 'leaky' in nature. Academic spinouts, a desirable output of university entrepreneurial ecosystems destined to lead to local/regional economic development, may not stay to fulfil their hypothesised promise. This is especially important when considering direct employment of quality human capital and spending within local university entrepreneurial ecosystems. Whilst most firms clearly stay, a good fifth of academic spinouts end up contributing to other regions' economic development efforts. Unfortunately, a great portion of that contribution flows towards the core regions, which are already doing well in economic terms. This leaves peripheral regions, which tend to exist in greater numbers across most nations, with a difficult situation to resolve: how to prevent the leakage? This is not just a case of invested efforts and resources into developing any single spinout company, but also a case of what happens later and where the uncoupling (see Chapter 4) delivers additional impact to develop university entrepreneurial ecosystems.

Policymakers keen on improving local gains from the activity of university entrepreneurial ecosystems need to pay close attention to the needs of academic spinouts, in order to identify retention factors and avoid pushing them to other regions. At the same time, whilst this 'leaky localism' of university entrepreneurial ecosystems presents itself as a zero-sum game, where one region gains as another loses firms, policymakers need to reflect on broader long-term effects that may be positive for all regions. As the migrant academic spinouts spread their spatial presence, they retain links with parent university entrepreneurial ecosystems. Consequently, they may enhance spatially distant networks of parent university entrepreneurial ecosystems, potentially leading to greater long-term returns. These may materialise through greater access to new ecosystemic actors and elements not present locally, which may amplify entrepreneurship activity locally, by diversifying and enriching university entrepreneurial ecosystems. Whilst severing local networks is a possible threat for most relocating firms (Atakhan-Kenneweg et al. 2021), for academic spinout companies this may be a lesser concern, given that central university entrepreneurial ecosystem actors – the universities – retain equity stakes in their spinout companies, representing strong, and potentially difficult to sever, network links.

CONCLUSION

From the findings presented in this chapter, it is clear that university entrepreneurial ecosystems are characterised by 'leaky localism', where they not only form networks that reach externally to other university entrepreneurial ecosystems (Prokop and Thompson 2023) and receive in-migration of firms, but also observe emigration of academic spinouts to other place-based entrepreneurial ecosystems. This leakage is not portrayed here as necessarily negative, even though at first it may present itself as loss of knowledge, human capital, and consequently economic growth potential. This leakage instead may result in the strengthening of university entrepreneurial ecosystem networks and the ability to spatially cast a wider 'relational' net, reinforcing university entrepreneurial ecosystem performance by enabling its spinout firms to tap into resources, cultures, and institutions present elsewhere that perhaps were not available within the parent university entrepreneurial ecosystem.

9. Boundaries of ecosystems

The geographical organisation of entrepreneurial ecosystems has pointed to cities and regions being the key spatial units within which ecosystems emerge and thrive. This spatially bounded character has become questionable with emerging work on university entrepreneurial ecosystems finding that to achieve compositional completeness they may form connections with actors outside their immediate locale. The aim of this chapter is to consider the issue of boundary of an ecosystem by focusing on the unique spatial organisation of university entrepreneurial ecosystems. The chapter begins by discussing the boundary problem and develops a typology of ecosystem boundaries that emerge from studies of university entrepreneurial ecosystems. The implications of discussions that follow highlight principally methodological and theoretical challenges, but also problems for policymakers in supporting and observing constructs that reveal a high degree of complexity.

THE CONCEPTUAL PROBLEMS OF A CLOSED BOUNDARY MODEL

The emergence of an entrepreneurial ecosystem is theorised as predicated on development of coherence among spatially proximate actors (Colombelli et al. 2019), which ensures common culture, and institutions governing self-organisation of entrepreneurial ecosystems (Roundy et al. 2018). This coherence leads to the development of homophily among ecosystem actors, which relies on commonalities and is more likely to have a proximate or localised character (Prokop and Thompson 2023). Indeed, many cases of entrepreneurial ecosystems (Brown and Mason 2017) and their evolutionary models (Mack and Mayer 2016; Colombelli et al. 2019) imagine a spatially bounded structure. However, these spatially contained models have recently began to attract critique for not observing the boundary aspects more carefully (Schäfer 2021). University entrepreneurial ecosystems appear to break this conceptual stereotype and reveal that their ecosystem organisation may include actors not present locally or proximately (Prokop 2021).

Whilst the key reason for non-local spatial organisation can be sought in pragmatism stemming from limitations of a place – and hence adding/borrowing elements to complete an ecosystem composition from other places – there may be alternative explanations. For example, university entrepreneurial ecosystems may develop organically outside of the perimeter of a particular place (e.g. through relocation of their spinouts, as depicted in Chapter 8), by following the emergence of coherence that is fundamentally based on networks. These networks may already be non-local in nature and the coherence may be achieved at a wider spatial level than just a single town or city. This is partly supported by works of Schäfer and Henn (2018) studying migrating entrepreneurs who influence these inter-ecosystem connections.

Importantly, since cluster literature theoretically underpins much of the thinking on entrepreneurial ecosystems (Spigel and Harrison 2018), networks have become automatically perceived as spatially proximate, and consequently place-bounded (Brown and Mason 2017). However, work that followed relational space (e.g. Binz et al. 2014) showed that a system may exist beyond a place, and in fact, proximity is not necessarily a pre-requisite for spatial organisation of actors. In fact, entrepreneurial ecosystems, just like technology innovation systems, may follow even an international organisation. This may be more likely for university entrepreneurial ecosystems that focus on high-end innovation activity, where related actors and communities that understand the nature of such derived ventures (i.e. academic spinouts) and their technologies may exist in scarcity and be unavailable locally.

Cluster-based thinking borrowed by the entrepreneurial ecosystems literature also suggests the presence of sectorally specialised concentration of firms or localised knowledge spillovers (Spigel and Harrison 2018). Whilst these aspects may be indeed observed in sectoral entrepreneurial ecosystems, university entrepreneurial ecosystems appear to show a different nature. First, as presented in Chapter 8, a substantial portion of academic spinout companies does not remain local; in fact these firms migrate to other regions. Consequently, the knowledge spillovers they engage in lose proximate character (beyond formation of a spinout company). Second, there is no specific sectoral – or science – bias present in university entrepreneurial ecosystems (Prokop et al. 2019), largely because universities engaged in research commercialisation lead wide spectra of knowledge generation across multiple fields. Unlike the evidence coming from sectoral entrepreneurial ecosystems (e.g. Berman et al. 2022), university entrepreneurial ecosystems appear to be sector-agnostic.

Another key argument for place-boundedness of an entrepreneurial ecosystem may be in its two key components: institutions and culture (Malecki 2018; Roundy et al. 2018). It follows that when ecosystems emerge and coherence increases among actors their increasingly homophilious or homogeneous culture and institutions remain at a local and bounded geographical level. There is good evidence that indeed institutions and culture are place-specific (Rodríguez-Pose 2020; Huggins and Thompson 2015), and as such different across places and territories to the extent where these may exert pressure on economic development outcomes. This may be quite important to a concept of a place-based entrepreneurial ecosystem or a nested ecosystem (Chapter 5).

However, as argued in this book, nested entrepreneurial ecosystems are a special case, and the likelihood is that rather than following proximity-based explanations, university entrepreneurial ecosystems are more likely to organise across relational and non-local space. There is a good reason for this. As academics tend to develop networks that have expertise in narrow fields of knowledge, their networks are more likely to follow spatial organisation of technology innovation systems (Binz et al. 2014) rather than clusters. Evidence for this can be found in the literature following university–industry collaborations (Huggins et al. 2010), where industry networks are critical for spinout formation (Prokop and Thompson 2023). These studies show that firms collaborating with universities tend to follow the latest and best science, wherever it is (Huggins et al. 2019). For example, the London (UK) based IP Group, a venture capital company investing in academic spinout companies, started by working with Oxford University, and subsequently by building links with key universities across the UK (e.g. Cardiff, Sheffield) and outside, in the US (e.g. Columbia University) or other countries. This may suggest that institutions and culture are either more homogenous within such emergent university entrepreneurial ecosystems, or more likely, the premise of university entrepreneurial ecosystems is centred on diversity, which includes the mixing of actors from different institutional and cultural backgrounds, but working towards common goals.

The spatially bounded character of ecosystems enables methodological parsimony, where it is easier to tie an ecosystem to a place, examine it and compare. This carries multiple advantages in defining actors and measuring inputs, outputs and outcomes – especially when considering subnational statistical data available at different scales of administrative boundaries (Schäfer 2021), identifying components of culture and institutions, and studying local networks. This may be particularly beneficial in promoting engagement of policymakers, enabling clearer areas for policy interventions and a possibility for monitoring results. Unfortunately, whilst a larger part of an ecosystem may be place-bounded, such methodological assumptions impose a particular perception of reality rather than depicting it accurately. The consequences may manifest themselves in poorer theorisation of ecosystems – which already suffer from such critique (Wurth et al. 2022; Brown and Mason 2017), and, instead of decreasing, increasing 'policy > inputs > outputs > outcomes' mismatch, leading to confusing results.

University entrepreneurial ecosystems and other sub-ecosystems offer a sufficient focus to disentangle the complexities of ecosystems, as such offering a way to resolve some of the theoretical issues of place-based entrepreneurial ecosystems. In what follows, I present how university entrepreneurial ecosystems challenge conceptualising of boundaries, and why the future of the ecosystems literature, in main part the university entrepreneurial ecosystems one, needs to be open to accurate depictions of the reality of ecosystems, even if it is very complex to capture.

WHICH UNIVERSITY ENTREPRENEURIAL ECOSYSTEMS HAVE AN OPEN CHARACTER?

It is more likely that spatially bounded university entrepreneurial ecosystems will be found in large urban areas, potentially in global cities, such as London, New York, Paris, Beijing or Tokyo. In such significant urban agglomerations there is a very high likelihood that any entrepreneurial ecosystem would be able to achieve compositional completeness employing actors present within. The remaining spectrum of university towns and cities may struggle to achieve compositional completeness with actors available locally; as such they may show a different degree of configuration and openness, revealing a multitude of diverse ecosystem forms (Spigel 2020).

For example, university entrepreneurial ecosystems based in small urban areas, such as the example of Scottish University Entrepreneurial Ecosystem described in Prokop (2021), are restricted by their surroundings, even though their key actors – the university and technology transfer office – may be a supporting foundation of a healthy number of new academic spinouts based on excellent research. For such ecosystems the specialist management team talent, entrepreneurial finance, and other actors are only available elsewhere, even hundreds of miles away. It is the conscious effort of the key actors that results in building connections to actors located in other urban areas in Scotland but also in Oxfordshire – a cluster of high technology entrepreneurship – which enables the Scottish University Entrepreneurial Ecosystem to achieve completeness. This is unique on a number of levels and contradictory to extant theorisations of entrepreneurial ecosystems, as highlighted in the previous section.

First, locally developed coherence, culture and institutions are clearly mixed with those from other places. Their mixing overcomes ecosystem's compositional limitations. It could be that such mixing is more likely to happen within a single national context, where nationally much of the culture and institutions are shared. At the same time, this negates the proximity arguments (Roundy et al. 2018) and shows a possibility of a more complex spatial organisation of entrepreneurial ecosystems. Second, it depicts how elements important to the functioning of an entrepreneurial ecosystem can be sourced from non-local areas. Given that university entrepreneurial ecosystems rely on commercialising the latest and highly specialised knowledge, they would naturally become organised around the actors, wherever these are available, rather than the boundary of a place, regardless of what actors are available. As such, the Scottish University Entrepreneurial Ecosystem described above shows that the quality of composition is more important than its proximity. Third, the example presented shows that the boundary of a university entrepreneurial ecosystem, and consequently any ecosystem, can be interregional and spatially unbound. This complexity does not make a university entrepreneurial ecosystem easier to understand, but it shows how determined its key actors are to resolve the weaknesses resulting from conditions beyond their control – i.e. the nature of the surroundings, so inherently critical to the entrepreneurial ecosystems concept (e.g. Stam 2015), but not attracting sufficient theoretical attention (Schäfer 2021).

Whilst Prokop (2021) does not depict the Scottish University Entrepreneurial Ecosystem as performing optimally, other well-performing cases are described: the Midlands University Entrepreneurial Ecosystem and the Wales University Entrepreneurial Ecosystem also follow spatial organisation that is non-local. In fact, many university entrepreneurial ecosystems stress their wider connections, such as Stanford University (2024) in the US, or ETH Zürich (ETH 2024) in Switzerland, revealing a reality that is complex, but designed to serve the demands of such dynamic structures. In their study of migrant entrepreneurs Schäfer and Henn (2018) captured one of the ways in which any entrepreneurial ecosystem may spread its networks beyond a single place. A naturally occurring movement of talent and entrepreneurs leads to the development of these linkages. As presented in Chapter 8, the relocation of academic spinouts may be contributing to this activity, as may the spatial availability of key actors.

All university entrepreneurial ecosystems have a possibility of developing an open character. Their specific composition and configuration may be dependent on locally available actors and those that are willing to ignore geographical distance as an impossible barrier. Whilst there are clear benefits to proximity, clearly not all actors of an ecosystem need to be local. It is important to stress that spatially bounded ecosystems are possible, but such spatial organisation may not be necessarily widespread.

THE BOUNDARY TYPOLOGY OF ECOSYSTEMS

In order to begin considerations of university entrepreneurial ecosystems that are in part defined by their place, but may be spatially open, it is important to distinguish between the spatial character of ecosystem actors and their roles. From discussions contained in previous chapters and examples described above, it is possible to identify three types of actors that make up university entrepreneurial ecosystems: (a) *core* ecosystem elements; (b) *functional* actors; and (c) *peripheral* ones.

For each university entrepreneurial ecosystem, the *core* actors are universities, technology transfer offices and academic spinout companies (including their entrepreneurs), but also elements such as institutions, culture, and networks, which align with Stam and Van de Ven's (2021) model (Prokop and Thompson 2023). These are integral components. The remaining actors can be located on a spectrum of probabilities whether they could be local or not. As such, it is posited here that any ecosystem is composed of a *core* which binds it to a key place, but does not restrict it to that place. Instead, the nature of the local area (e.g. the level of agglomeration economies) and the location of remaining actors are what determine the degree of spatial boundedness. Here culture and institutions may tend towards coherence within an ecosystem characterised by a high degree of spatial boundedness, and tend towards greater diversity within ecosystems of a low degree of spatial boundedness. The level of mixing of these actors/elements, their ability to form effective configurations, will determine the outputs and outcomes of each university entrepreneurial ecosystem. It may be that the exact same spatial organisation of two university entrepreneurial ecosystems generates different outputs and outcomes, because their actors function differently, or the cultures and institutions they connect either blend well, to a different degree, or do not mix at all.

The *core* of a university entrepreneurial ecosystem defines its place-character, but does not impose place boundaries on it. The *core* is, however, place-bounded itself. The remaining parts of the ecosystem are integral to its optimal performance, and whilst not *core*, cannot also be regarded as *peripheral*. These are *functional* actors. They may be either local or non-local, and define the degree of spatial boundedness of an entrepreneurial ecosystem. For university entrepreneurial ecosystems these actors could constitute the industry, investors, science parks, accelerators and business incubators, but also the management talent. Their actual spatial character cannot be pre-defined, rather it needs to be observed. *Functional* actors do not determine place-belonging of any ecosystem, but are critical to the optimal functioning of an ecosystem, since they enable it to reach compositional completeness. These may also involve culture and institutions that differ from the *core* elements, even though all actors and elements would be working towards the same goal: improving entrepreneurship activity. Importantly, *core* elements of university entrepreneurial ecosystems have an ability to establish *functional* actors themselves (e.g. science parks, university seed funds), but the likelihood that *functional* actors would establish *core* elements is minimal.

Peripheral actors and elements enrich a university entrepreneurial ecosystem that is already complete, but are not a substitute for *core* or *functional* components. Chapter 5 on levels of ecosystems has captured these *peripheral* actors as operational ones. They can be considered as replicative in character for each actor type. For example, a university entrepreneurial ecosystem that already has investors in its composition, may connect to further investors. These are additional actors to *core* and *functional* ones, adding further variety, reach, and capacity to enrich university entrepreneurial ecosystems. Crucially, *peripheral* actors may have both local and non-local character, but there is a higher likelihood that they will be non-local, as it may be difficult to identify more than one actor locally for certain actor types across towns and smaller cities (e.g. science parks, business incubators). This likelihood increases even further if *functional* actors are already non-local.

A keen reader may ask now: how to determine which element is *functional* and which is *peripheral*? Indeed, this is an important distinction. Drawing from network theory on the strength of ties (Granovetter 1973), *functional* actors could be determined as those that form the strongest link with the *core* elements. Conversely, *peripheral* actors are more likely to form weaker links with *core* elements. However, it is important to stress that some university entrepreneurial ecosystems may have replicative *functional* actors, with equal strength of connections. The probability of such setups would be greater in highly agglomerated urban areas characterised by a munificence of ecosystemic actors and a higher concentration of network capital (Huggins 2010). For most university entrepreneurial ecosystems, and especially those tied to smaller urban areas such as towns, *functional* actors would have a lower probability of containing replicative actors. Ecosystems can access these from within a single place – from other sub-ecosystems – or from other ecosystems (i.e. located elsewhere).

Since the spatial organisation of university entrepreneurial ecosystems would be determined by the *functional* actors, it is possible to distinguish two key ecosystem types, based on the nature of their boundaries: *closed* and *open* ecosystems. *Closed* ecosystems have been widely depicted in the literature; these are ecosystems where *functional* actors would be co-located with *core* elements. These are also more likely to follow a nested character (Chapter 5), given the pre-requisite for all key actors to be contained in a place. Conversely, *open* ecosystems build connections that are non-local. Here, at least one of the *functional* actors needs to be based in a different place than the *core* elements of the ecosystem. Whilst one could determine the degree of openness or spatial boundedness by studying how many *functional* elements are local vs. non-local, without empirical investigation linking of this character to outputs and/or outcomes it is difficult to speculate on its impact on the performance of an ecosystem.

Both *closed* and *open* ecosystems may include *peripheral* actors. The location of *peripheral* actors should have a lesser degree of influence on the performance of any ecosystem, although their importance cannot be excluded, as their presence would otherwise be redundant. For both *closed* and *open* ecosystems the *functional* actors are *responsible* for the optimal performance of the ecosystem reflected in outputs, such as new firms formed and their success, as well as outcomes in terms of local economic development. Figures 9.1 and 9.2 illustrate the *closed* and *open* ecosystem types, respectively.

University Entrepreneurial Ecosystem A is a *closed* ecosystem. It contains its *core* elements and *functional* actors within the boundaries of a place the university is anchored to. The *peripheral* actors of the university entrepreneurial ecosystem may be drawn from a local area, but are more likely to have a non-local character.

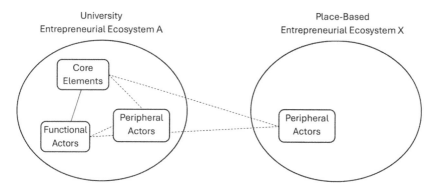

Note: Continuous lines represent strong ties, dotted lines depict weak ties.

Figure 9.1   Closed model of university entrepreneurial ecosystem

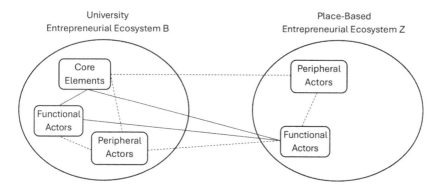

Note: Continuous lines represent strong ties, dotted lines depict weak ties.

Figure 9.2   Open model of university entrepreneurial ecosystem

Conversely, as University Entrepreneurial Ecosystem B has an *open* character, its *functional* actors may be both local and non-local, as at least one of them is located outside the university's place. Similarly, *peripheral* actors can be accessed both locally, if they replicate the types of *functional* actors already present locally and strongly connected to the *core* elements, and non-locally.

In both cases, *open* and *closed*, *peripheral* actors can be connected to both the *core* elements and/or *functional* elements. Given the literature's indication of network connections and homogeneity development (e.g. Colombelli et al. 2019) – the coherence – it is more likely that these links will exist between all different actor types, rather than just the *core* and *peripheral* or *functional* and *peripheral*.

IMPLICATIONS FOR FUTURE RESEARCH

Defining the boundaries of university entrepreneurial ecosystems, and more broadly any entrepreneurial ecosystem, is difficult and poses methodological challenges for studying ecosystems. Whilst this chapter responds to the critique advanced in Schäfer (2021), it does not offer a comprehensive typology. However, it shows that it is important to define and acknowledge the nature of ecosystem boundaries. Without doing so, many studies may end up depicting local fragments of ecosystems, but not the ecosystem itself, its spatial extent, or complexity.

Applying the dichotomous framework proposed here is a first step towards building a clearer theory of university entrepreneurial ecosystems. Future scholars of university entrepreneurial ecosystems, and those of wider ecosystems inspired by this chapter, may be influenced to design methodologies for empirical studies that expect some level of non-local sprawl of an ecosystem. By examining for the presence of such actors, either *functional* or *peripheral*, scholars can define the boundaries of ecosystems, and in so doing present the variety of ecosystem designs, their unique configurations and spatial organisation. In so doing, the literature may aim closer towards a more effective and precise theory of entrepreneurial ecosystems.

It is important to note that there may be more diverse forms of ecosystem boundaries not depicted here. Future research may focus on exploring these, and defining their models, building on the framework presented above. Importantly, studies that will link the types of ecosystem boundaries to outputs and outcomes may bring in a set of fresh perspectives on the importance of boundaries, and specific boundary types. There is also a need for future research to design methodologies and metrics to define and measure boundaries, in order to simplify embedding them in empirical efforts, especially those of quantitative and/or comparative character.

IMPLICATIONS FOR POLICY

There is an inherent challenge for local and central policymakers in dealing with increasingly complex theories, as it may lead to a need for more intricate and sophisticated policy designs. These may be untested and potentially result in undesirable and unexpected outcomes. However, a good start for the local policymakers is in acknowledging the existence of different boundary models and recognising that the ecosystems they try to support or develop may have a higher or lower probability of being open. In essence, the openness cannot be regarded merely as a threat to local economic development, a leakage of outputs, but rather as a two-way flow, with positive output gains from other places.

This open character poses challenges in comparing and measuring university entrepreneurial ecosystems for central policymakers. Tracking how each ecosystem contributes to the economic development level at subnational territorial scale becomes difficult, when that contribution is spread across more than one place. Defining boundaries and types of actors may assist policymakers in attributing outputs, but essentially new methodologies and statistical data collection efforts are required to measure outcomes accurately. By overcoming this challenge, comparisons of university entrepreneurial ecosystems can be advanced, aiding precision of policy designs.

It is important to note that university entrepreneurial ecosystems are unique structures, that reveal a variety of spatial organisations and functional configurations, and consequently outputs and outcomes. With the development of the literature and evidence base, understanding causalities between ecosystem designs and their performance may better inform future policy designs. In the meantime, this complexity needs to be interpreted very carefully by policymakers, in particular, to avoid following the best-practice trap in designing policy interventions, which may waste resources by delivering undesirable outcomes.

University policies could be revised to promote more collaborative approaches, sharing resources and developing support across university entrepreneurial ecosystems. A collaborative or more centralised approach was suggested in the past (Degroof and Roberts 2004), but little progress has been made in this direction. There is a particular predicament in higher education, where universities tend to operate independently, which is important to their individual reputations and organisational outcomes. However, the nature of university entrepreneurial ecosystems is collaborative, and central policymakers could play a role in stimulating closer partnerships between universities to build better performing university entrepreneurial ecosystems that generate economic benefits to wider areas.

CONCLUSION

This chapter took on a challenging task of addressing the problem of bound-aries in university entrepreneurial ecosystems. The bulk of the literature on entrepreneurial ecosystems assumes their place-boundedness (e.g. Malecki 2018; Roundy et al. 2018), indicating the importance of homogenous culture and institutions developed in places rather than across places (Roundy 2016). Such studies investigate ecosystems as restricted to a geographical place (e.g. Spigel and Vinodrai 2020; Miller and Acs 2017), yet evidence suggests that actors not present in an ecosystem's immediate geographical and bounded space – as evidenced through university entrepreneurial ecosystems (Prokop 2021) – may form an active ecosystem that goes beyond simple administrative boundaries (Schäfer 2021). This boundary setting merely enables studies of ecosystems to be manageable, but not necessarily true reflections of their spatial span and configuration. University entrepreneurial ecosystems enable observation of how actors are drawn from outside a local geography, perhaps because their key actors – universities – have a long history of operating and collaborating in an unbounded geographical space (Huggins et al. 2020), with their economic development contribution reflecting this character.

The two models of university entrepreneurial ecosystems presented above – *open* and *closed* – enable clearer delineation of where the ecosystem's boundary could be, and how it should be defined. Whilst no metrics are sug-gested, the chapter sketches out ways to think about studying the boundaries of university entrepreneurial ecosystems. Importantly, despite the focus on university entrepreneurial ecosystems, the conceptual thinking behind bound-aries lends itself to a wider application to larger place-based entrepreneurial ecosystems. Importantly, this chapter shows how insights from other parts of this book come together, how they fit, even though they present separate aspects of university entrepreneurial ecosystems. Lastly, for a comprehensive theory of university entrepreneurial ecosystems, one that captures their inher-ent complexity and non-linearity, defining what happens within and outside of places where we find universities is particularly crucial, as it challenges the parsimony of spatial boundedness and improves our understanding of a wider role and impact of universities and the ecosystems they form.

10. Conclusion: university entrepreneurial ecosystems and asymmetry of opportunities

This book has devoted substantial attention to university entrepreneurial eco-systems. In doing so, it exposed the unique importance of these ecosystems, the reasons why they should be treated separately, and why all sub-ecosystems are important constructs to understand entrepreneurial activity occurring within a place. Specifically, university entrepreneurial ecosystems translate knowledge generated at their core actor, the university, into high-technology entrepreneurial activity that is critical to economic development of places and nations more widely. Whilst much scholarly effort has recognised the impor-tance of university commercialisation activity, only very limited work has attempted to link this activity to contextual conditions, networks of actors that support high-technology and high-risk enterprises, and shown how an ecosys-tem made up of multiple previously individually studied elements and actors, networks, institutions and culture results in new academic spinout companies being created and sustained in their development towards major companies.

The literature on entrepreneurial ecosystems has been instrumental in chan-nelling the thinking that went into this book, granting theoretical space to the geography of the university, but also recognising its ecosystem. At the same time, studying university entrepreneurial ecosystems incidentally revealed many theoretical challenges of the wider entrepreneurial ecosystems literature, as highlighted across the past chapters. This is a positive development, as many advances made towards a theory of university entrepreneurial ecosys-tems would inherently be linked to the wider entrepreneurial ecosystems, and vice versa. However, this is not to suggest that university entrepreneurial eco-systems are the same as entrepreneurial ecosystems. This book has hopefully presented a compelling case to convince the reader that university entrepre-neurial ecosystems are unique, they are understudied and consequently their potentially world-changing enterprises cannot be merely drowned in a more generic pool of wider entrepreneurial ecosystem outputs, but rather can be linked to specific inputs, institutions, culture and supporting elements and actors that do not generate any other forms of entrepreneurship.

Consequently, the focus of this book was on academic spinouts as the key outputs of university entrepreneurial ecosystems. These are companies of a special type, created in conditions that most companies are not, and as such are a mark of recognition of a live university entrepreneurial ecosystem. Whilst universities are also responsible for student entrepreneurship and graduate start-ups, these forms of entrepreneurship are inherently not that different from a general population of firms, in that they represent a similar broad distribution of types of firms: from non-technology to technology-based, not all directly attributed to employing the latest university-generated knowledge. As such, they may indeed be part of a parallel campus ecosystem (Miller and Acs 2017), but they do not capture the characteristics of academic spinout companies, nor the organised and partly dedicated setup of actors and elements supporting them.

The discussions covered in previous chapters point out the very complex nature of university entrepreneurial ecosystems. Each such ecosystem appears to be independently and uniquely designed and configured, but crucially not all of them generate the same level of outputs in terms of numbers of academic spinouts that grow into successful companies and survive over a longer period of time. The remaining parts of this chapter are devoted to synthesising discussions contained in this book by focusing on a key emergent challenge these highlight: the asymmetry of opportunities.

THE ASYMMETRY OF OPPORTUNITIES

University entrepreneurial ecosystems reveal a variety of compositions, contexts, configurations, outputs, and outcomes. Crucially, the individual and independent character of university entrepreneurial ecosystems underlines asymmetric opportunities available to academic entrepreneurs across the spectrum of these ecosystems. For academics that intend to start up spinout companies, this carries as much weight as for the local economic development of places their universities are anchored to. I consider three key sources of these asymmetries: (a) geography; (b) networks; and (c) university entrepreneurial ecosystems.

Geography

The spatial context of university entrepreneurial ecosystems determines the munificence of resources, actors, and elements available. In particular, larger urban agglomerations may contain a greater variety of actors that may specialise in supporting academic spinout companies, compared with areas where many such actors may simply not exist. For universities based in small towns and remote areas, this may signify the importance of the spatial reorganisation of their ecosystems, in order to maximise compositional completeness. It is a response to the inequality of opportunities available to these ecosystems in a place they are anchored to. To overcome this asymmetry, some university entrepreneurial ecosystems make an effort to reorganise their designs to improve compositional completeness, but also to access additional actors that may enable them to enrich the level of support and opportunities offered to academic spinout companies. This changes the character of the university entrepreneurial ecosystems, from the originally perceived closed systems expressed in spatial boundedness to open ones, where the university town or city no longer limits the ecosystem's development. Such complex organisation that is partly decoupled from its place aims to redefine the level of opportunities afforded by its local geography.

These opportunities may be identified through access to specialist human capital, such as talented management teams that have experience in developing science-based ventures, but also skilled researchers that have expertise in a very narrow and often novel field. Whilst traditionally, academic spinouts may have drawn on resources available from the parent university or its ecosystem, in their scarcity, such companies may try to find them elsewhere.

As such, academic spinout companies also reorganise their geography by relocating to other places or ecosystems (Chapter 8). The significant volume of such migrations highlights the uneven distribution of perceived opportunities that academic spinout companies identify as important to access. That is, it is important enough to commit to moving costs and a potential severing of existing network ties in order to realise benefits available elsewhere. The evidence presented here suggests that this effort may indeed result in the equalising of some opportunities (e.g. access to finance). However, relocation of academic spinouts requires more insight, as the process of embedding into a new spatial context (including building of new networks, dealing with logistics, available human capital, institutions, and culture, etc.) may erase all of the benefits of doing so. In other words, even if companies improve their access to finance, they may end up unable to employ it effectively to secure their success.

As sub-ecosystems, university entrepreneurial ecosystems reveal a unique possibility of co-existing within a single city or town (Chapter 3) and not just across places. This nature shows the disconnect between university entrepreneurial ecosystems, and how their spatial circumstances are made more complex by the strong individual and independent nature of such ecosystems. Consequently, the asymmetry of opportunities presents itself as a complex intra- and inter-territorial problem of university entrepreneurial ecosystems, an idiosyncratic issue that does not feature in the wider entrepreneurial ecosystems literature.

Networks

University entrepreneurial ecosystems form networks of different character, density, centrality, closure, and structural holes, leading to variable levels of opportunities arising from such relational configurations (Chapter 5), and resulting in a broad spectrum of performance in forming academic spinout companies and sustaining their growth. This is in part captured by the availability of actors and spatial organisation of university entrepreneurial ecosystems, but also the ability to adjust network positions of ecosystem actors, either through building connections or strengthening them. This complexity and diversity of underlying network architectures underpinning university entrepreneurial ecosystems leave academic spinout companies with an uneven access to opportunities, where even in two similarly composed ecosystems, firms may experience different capabilities to employ available resources.

This may be reinforced by local culture and institutions of places the university entrepreneurial ecosystems are tied to, which may make even the most densely connected ecosystems ineffective, if their actors operate on low levels of trust or are constrained by formal institutions. As such, networks cannot be considered independently of other elements of university entrepreneurial ecosystems, since their functioning determines the availability of opportunities at an ecosystem level. Concomitantly, networks are further tied to place characteristics, with regions revealing different entrepreneurial natures (Prokop and Kitagawa 2022). In fact, it is highly likely that the asymmetry of opportunities stemming from networks may reflect the economic structure and level of success of regions and localities (Huggins and Prokop 2017). For example, when a university entrepreneurial ecosystem exists in an economically core region where industry networks include many key companies that are strongly connected within and outside the region, the opportunities presented to academic spinouts in such circumstances may be superior to those offered in regions with poorly connected networks or ones that do not include many well-performing (anchor tenant) companies. These opportunities could be realised through greater access to sophisticated and well-resourced markets, but also technologically advanced and flexible suppliers, or distribution specialists.

University Entrepreneurial Ecosystems

The university, the key actor of each university entrepreneurial ecosystem (Chapter 2), is a very specific construct with a unique history, culture, resources, mix of missions, administrative efficiency, and specialist focus in fields of knowledge that represents the capture of an inimitable academic talent. Importantly, universities cannot exist without their faculty, as academics develop new knowledge, disseminate it through publications and teaching, and commercialise it. Given that some universities are more focused on teaching, there is an expectation that such institutions will indeed generate lower volumes of academic spinouts, if any at all, as disclosures based on research are the underlying prerequisite to develop such firms (Prokop and Thompson 2023). Consequently, the asymmetry of opportunities starts at the very source of academic spinouts.

Furthermore, universities are the ecosystem's transforming agents. They are responsible for developing their own ecosystems, creating technology transfer offices, organising access to business incubators, science parks, early stage funding, and spinout mentorship schemes, and building connections or partnerships with other functional and peripheral actors. This is a vastly different nature from one promoted in the wider entrepreneurial ecosystems literature – where such agency is distributed across a wider set of actors. As such, depending on the university needs, policies, strategies, and resources university entrepreneurial ecosystems may evolve into variable compositions and configurations. This in turn leaves every academic entrepreneur initially bound to an ecosystem that may predefine their venture's success, and in the worst circumstances lead it to early and potentially avoidable failure.

This asymmetry of opportunities is further reinforced through the commercialisation experience and culture of the departments at universities, but also universities as wider institutions. For example, there are many cases reported in the literature where chairs of departments supportive of commercialisation activity are critical to encouraging their colleagues to explore commercial potential of knowledge they generate (Bercovitz and Feldman 2008). Similarly, universities may create institutions that either ease this activity or make it more difficult, depending on the value they place on knowledge commercialisation, and whether they align it with academic promotion criteria. It is well known that at most universities promotion (and tenure) is granted predominantly based on research outputs, and even when impact activities are included, these may not receive an equal consideration. Consequently, university entrepreneurial ecosystems that perform particularly well in forming academic spinouts could be ones that offer greater recognition to this activity, in essence having developed more enabling institutions.

Having outlined some of the key asymmetries of opportunities that emerged from discussions across this book, the next section attempts to respond to them. There are no easy formulas to do so, and it is important to remember that best practice cases may often lead to poor outcomes if transplanted. The agents of change in university entrepreneurial ecosystems need to be careful in setting evolutionary paths for their ecosystems. New paths should be uniquely resolving asymmetries of each university entrepreneurial ecosystem, based on understanding of its composition, configuration, and spatial organisation.

HOW TO RESOLVE THESE ASYMMETRIES?

Economic geography is a field concerned with asymmetries of opportunities across places, and with university entrepreneurial ecosystems it enables thinking beyond a single ecosystem's case, recognising the complexity of solutions and their need to fit individual circumstances. In fact, some of these solutions may need to resolve intra-place asymmetries, revealing how a city or town may represent a challenging geographical space for university entrepreneurial ecosystems.

By recognising the asymmetry of opportunities, a number of recommendations can be advanced to guide stakeholders of university entrepreneurial ecosystems towards solution-oriented reflections. I present these below, acknowledging that these may not be recipes, but rather broader considerations. With the advances in theorising university entrepreneurial ecosystems, it is hoped that recipes may emerge.

University entrepreneurial ecosystems, and specifically their key agents – the universities – need to carefully observe their entrepreneurial outputs, and if possible compare with other similar ecosystems (Chapter 6). Finding an optimum calibration model will influence the performance of ecosystems. Critically, outputs of university entrepreneurial ecosystems are strongly related to their composition and filtration. It is important to observe if enough academic spinouts are being set up in relation to resources and support available at the ecosystem, but also to identify if similar inputs (as in other university entrepreneurial ecosystems) generate different outputs. Whilst in itself this may not solve any problems, it may reaffirm good performance or highlight a need to reassess the composition, filtration, and configuration of these in the university entrepreneurial ecosystem. Across a number of countries there already exist sufficient data to capture some of these aspects, e.g. in the US there is the Association of University Technology Managers Licensing Activity Survey, in the UK equivalent data are collected through the Higher Education Business and Community Interaction survey. These can be employed to form the initial basis for such internal assessments, or external, if central policymakers recognise it as important to invest in the development of a state-of-the-art national commercialisation ecosystem by supporting university entrepreneurial ecosystems.

The place a university entrepreneurial ecosystem is tied to should not be its boundary (Chapter 9). Closed entrepreneurial ecosystems emerge in rare urban circumstances (large agglomerations), but no university entrepreneurial ecosystem should be closed. Clearly, opportunities are available in other places and accessing them may require a set of peripheral actors spread across different cities and towns that channel these to academic spinouts located in proximity to the core elements of university entrepreneurial ecosystems. These weak ties may contribute the one key opportunity that an academic spinout may need in order to spur its growth. As such, relocation of academic spinouts should not be viewed as necessarily negative, since it may result in building networks that a university entrepreneurial ecosystem could access in the future. Consequently, it is imperative that university entrepreneurial ecosystems maintain connections with their academic spinouts over a longer timeframe, even after the sale of equity.

The spatial organisation of university entrepreneurial ecosystems is a response to unfavourable local conditions. It is not necessarily an easy solution to place-based constraints imposed on ecosystems, as it requires the building of inter-territorial connections and investments in maintenance of networks that have a built-in distance component. Consequently, university entrepreneurial ecosystems may place emphasis on their technology transfer offices to be in charge of those, but crucially, should devote necessary and long-term resources to achieving this. To do so, it is necessary to identify that many such networks constitute the social capital of professionals working in technology transfer offices, and without their longer-term roles, these may easily disappear. Renewing or rebuilding networks may be more costly than retaining staff long-term.

In order to understand the performance of university entrepreneurial eco-systems, it is important to recognise that they are in constant flux and their organisation changes dynamically, reflecting the evolutionary trajectories of academic spinouts. Their outputs may suffer time lag issues, with the full impact of any changes being reflected in outputs captured in subsequent years. Efforts to correct asymmetries of opportunities need to account for this built-in complexity. Basing decisions that define new evolutionary paths for university entrepreneurial ecosystems on wrong evaluation of data may result in limited improvements and potentially reinforce the asymmetry of opportunities.

Whilst it is difficult to influence change of culture and institutions at a place level, university entrepreneurial ecosystems may work towards university-based policies that support academic entrepreneurship and the formation of academic spinouts. This could be achieved at university level, through a built-in mechanism to enable a release of time to focus on establishing spinout ventures (e.g. proof of concept development, prototyping, market research), without negative consequences for academic careers (regardless of the outcome in terms of spinout venture formation). At the same time, public research funding bodies should enable additional resources to examine commercial potential of outputs of each research project. Clearly, university entrepreneurial ecosystems are uniquely positioned to contribute to economic development, by engaging in transforming knowledge into economic output at its source (Chapter 7). The relevant change agents and supporting stakeholders need to acknowledge their role in ensuring that this process is formalised and available to all research outputs, rather than being an afterthought for the faculty performing research.

It is important to observe what happens to academic spinout companies when they become larger, fail or become successful (Chapter 4). In particular, university entrepreneurial ecosystems observing the uncoupling process need to identify strategies or mechanisms to capture recycling of entrepreneurs and the resources released during this cycle. This may be even more critical when academic spinouts relocate away from the core element of university entre-preneurial ecosystems, where such processes may be harder to capture. There is a substantial value in capturing the uncoupling stage, as it feeds the next evolutionary cycle within the university entrepreneurial ecosystems.

THE AGENDA FOR FUTURE RESEARCH

This book has tried to draw attention to university entrepreneurial ecosystems by highlighting their unique status. It has contributed to the theory of univer-sity entrepreneurial ecosystems, and in part to mainstream entrepreneurial ecosystems and economic geography literatures. However, given that the university entrepreneurial ecosystem is an emerging concept, the book uncov-ered a spectrum of questions that need to be answered in order to improve our understanding of these ecosystems.

Unfortunately, as with wider entrepreneurial ecosystems, I may leave the reader with an undertheorised concept. I hope that, at least, the extent of this undertheorisation is minimised and focused on further calibration of the concept. In what follows, I set an agenda for future researchers interested in pursuing the concept of university entrepreneurial ecosystems.

The book has defined university entrepreneurial ecosystems, but crucially, given the emergent nature of this concept, it may not have done so compre-hensively enough. Future studies should explore the extent of the concept by exploring new cases, comparing them, and establishing consistent inter-national metrics. Much can also be learnt from a broader examination of all entrepreneurial sub-ecosystems to further delineate the theoretical boundaries of each such structure.

Given the complex geography of university entrepreneurial ecosystems there is further scope to disentangle the problems of co-location of these ecosystems and examine cases where collaborative relationships between university entre-preneurial ecosystems are observed and what these mean for the performance of university entrepreneurial ecosystems. Critically, it is important to further understand the economic impact of university entrepreneurial ecosystems on the local areas they are tied to and other local areas their actors inhabit, and to discern between different spatial organisations of university entrepreneurial ecosystems and resultant impacts. In particular, scholars taking interest in the impact of university entrepreneurial ecosystems on rural and peripheral areas would draw attention to aspects typically ignored, but potentially important for policy.

The evolutionary aspects of university entrepreneurial ecosystems suggest a complex dimension that may affect how these are composed and configured. Research exploring academic spinouts at different stages could build on the model presented in Chapter 4. Studies of evolution of university entrepreneurial ecosystems and how their paths develop in relation to academic spinout success would be particularly insightful, given the intricate and complex nature of such processes.

Although the book tried to position university entrepreneurial ecosystems within a framework of sub-ecosystems, it may be that the hybrid ecosystems reveal further typologies. Empirical evidence that helps clarify and build this picture could be well positioned to contribute to debates on the university entrepreneurial ecosystem concept and the wider entrepreneurial ecosystems one.

University entrepreneurial ecosystems are economically unique in that they enable entrepreneurial activity at the source of knowledge generation. Entrepreneurial filter theory explains the mechanism through which university entrepreneurial ecosystems (and wider entrepreneurial ecosystems) influence the success of academic spinouts. Future research should uncover metrics and methods to define filtration across all stages of venture development. This may take a form of a composite index. Crucially, any method should have wider appeal to international audiences by employing metrics that can be reproduced across national contexts. Furthermore, understanding whether Prokop's filtration has a linear or non-linear character could add to clearer policymaking, university entrepreneurial ecosystem designs and configurations, as well as functionality and roles of actors at different ecosystem evolution stages.

The academic spinout relocation activity depicts a complex reality of university entrepreneurial ecosystems. There is a clear paucity of research exploring this aspect, in particular why academic spinouts relocate, what draws them to particular areas, and what are the specific push, pull, and retention factors unique to academic spinout companies. In uncovering these issues, our understanding of university entrepreneurial ecosystems, their places and surroundings, could become stronger.

Whilst boundaries of university entrepreneurial ecosystems expose a unique challenge in studying these structures, there is a need for empirical studies to identify how university entrepreneurial ecosystems and their unique boundaries are related to entrepreneurial outputs and economic development outcomes. For wider entrepreneurial ecosystems, depicting the real boundaries may enable clarity of the importance and economic implications of spatially bounded conceptualisation of ecosystems.

The agenda outlined above is not exhaustive, but it reflects the emerging nature of the concept, its importance, and impact. It shows the scale of work left to the academic and policy communities. It is hoped that in developing a deeper understanding of university entrepreneurial ecosystems, successful recipes can be formulated and shared widely, resulting in greater positive technological, economic, and societal impacts worldwide.

References

Aaboen, L., Laage-Hellman, J., Lind, F., Oberg, C. and Shih, T. 2016. Exploring the roles of university spin-offs in business networks. *Industrial Marketing Management* 59, 157–166.

Abreu, M. and Grinevich, V. 2013. The nature of academic entrepreneurship in the UK: widening the focus on entrepreneurial activities. *Research Policy* 42, 408–422.

Acs, Z., Plummer, L. A. and Sutter, R. 2009. Penetrating the knowledge filter in 'rust belt' economies. *Annals of Regional Science* 43, 989–1012.

Acs, Z. J. and Plummer, L. A. 2005. Penetrating the 'knowledge filter in regional economies. *Annals of Regional Science* 39, 439–456.

Acs, Z. J., Braunerhjelm, P., Audretsch, D. B. and Carlsson, B. 2009. The knowledge spillover theory of entrepreneurship. *Small Business Economics* 32, 15–30.

Acs, Z. J., Audretsch, D. B. and Lehmann, E. E. 2013. The knowledge spillover theory of entrepreneurship. *Small Business Economics* 41, 757–774.

Alaassar, A., Mention, A.-L. and Aas, T. H. 2022. Ecosystem dynamics: exploring the interplay within fintech entrepreneurial ecosystems. *Small Business Economics* 58, 2157–2182.

Aldridge, T. T. and Audretsch, D. 2011. The Bayh–Dole Act and scientist entrepreneurship. *Research Policy* 40(8), 1058–1067.

Alexander, A. T. and Martin, D. P. 2013. Intermediaries for open innovation: a competence-based comparison of knowledge transfer offices practices. *Technological Forecasting and Social Change* 80(1), 38–49.

Allahar, H. and Sookram, R. 2019. A university business school as an entrepreneurial ecosystem hub. *Technology Innovation Management Review* 9(11), 15–25.

Alvedalen, J. and Boschma, R. 2017. A critical review of entrepreneurial ecosystems research: towards a future research agenda. *European Planning Studies* 26(6), 887–903.

Alvedalen, J. and Carlsson, B. 2021. Scaling up in entrepreneurial ecosystems: a comparative study of Entrepreneurial Ecosystems in Life Sciences. Papers in Innovation Studies no. 2021/09, CIRCLE, Lund University.

Asheim, B. T. 1996. Industrial districts as 'learning regions': a condition for prosperity. *European Planning Studies* 4(4), 379–400.

Åstebro, T., Braunerhjelm, P. and Broström, A. 2013. Does academic entrepreneurship pay? *Industrial and Corporate Change* 22(1), 281–311.

Atakhan-Kenneweg, M., Oerlemans, L. A. G. and Raab, J. 2021. New interorganizational knowledge tie formation after firm relocation: investigating the impact of spatial, relational, and temporal context. *Journal of Business Research* 127, 264–276.

Audretsch, D. and Belitski, M. 2021. Frank Knight, uncertainty and knowledge spillover entrepreneurship. *Journal of Institutional Economics* 17(6), 1005–1031.

Audretsch, D. B. 2018. Entrepreneurship, economic growth, and geography. *Oxford Review of Economic Policy* 34(4), 637–651.

Audretsch, D. B. and Feldman, M. P. 1996. R&D spillovers and the geography of innovation and production. *American Economic Review* 86(3), 630–640.

Audretsch, D. B. and Lehmann, E. E. 2005. Does the knowledge spillover theory of entrepreneurship hold for regions? *Research Policy* 34(8), 1191–1202.

Audretsch, D. B., Aldridge, T. T. and Oettl, A. 2006. The knowledge filter and economic growth: the role of scientist entrepreneurship. Kauffman Foundation Large Research Projects Research.

Audretsch, D. B., Cunningham, J. A., Kuratko, D. F., Lehmann, E. E. and Menter, M. 2019. Entrepreneurial ecosystems: economic, technological, and societal impacts. *Journal of Technology Transfer* 44, 313–325.

Auerswald, P. E. and Dani, L. 2017. The adaptive life cycle of entrepreneurial ecosystems: the biotechnology cluster. *Small Business Economics* 49, 97–117.

Autio, E., Nambisan, S., Thomas, L. D. W. and Wright, M. 2018. Digital affordances, spatial affordances, and the genesis of entrepreneurial ecosystems. *Strategic Entrepreneurship Journal* 12(1), 72–95.

Avnimelech, G. and Feldman, M. P. 2015. The stickiness of university spinoffs: a study of forma and informal spinoffs and their location from 124 US academic institutions. *International Journal of Technology Management* 68(1/2), 122–149.

Bagchi-Sen, S., Baines, N. and Smith, H. L. 2022. Characteristics and outputs of university spin-offs in the United Kingdom. *International Regional Science Review* 45(6), 606–635.

Baldwin, R. E. and Okubo, T. 2006. Heterogeneous firms, agglomeration and economic geography: spatial selection and sorting. *Journal of Economic Geography* 6(3), 323–346.

Barbosa, N. and Faria, A. P. 2020. The effect of entrepreneurial origin on firms' performance: the case of Portuguese academic spinoffs. *Industrial and Corporate Change* 29(1), 25–42.

Barnes, W., Gartland, M. and Stack, M. 2004. Old habits die hard: path dependency and behavioral lock-in. *Journal of Economic Issues* 38(2), 371–377.

Becker, G. S. 1965. A theory of the allocation of time. *The Economic Journal* 75(299), 493–517.

Bekkers, R., Gilsing, V. and van der Steen, M. 2006. Determining factors of the effectiveness of IP-based spin-offs: comparing the Netherlands and the US. *Journal of Technology Transfer* 31, 545–566.

Benneworth, P. and Charles, D. 2005. University spin-off policies and economic development in less successful regions: learning from two decades of policy practice. *European Planning Studies* 13(4), 537–557.

Bercovitz, J. and Feldman, M. 2008. Academic entrepreneurs: organizational change at the individual level. *Organization Science* 19(1), 69–89.

Berggren, E. and Lindholm Dahlstrand, Å. 2009. Creating an entrepreneurial region: two waves of academic spin-offs from Halmstad University. *European Planning Studies* 17(8), 1171–1189.

Berman, A., Cano-Kollmann, M. and Mudambi, R. 2022. Innovation and entrepreneurial ecosystems: fintech in the financial services industry. *Review of Managerial Science* 16, 45–64.

Bertello, A., Battisti, E., De Bernardi, P. and Bresciani, S. 2022. An integrative framework of knowledge-intensive and sustainable entrepreneurship in entrepreneurial ecosystems. *Journal of Business Research* 142, 683–693.

Bichler, B. F., Kallmuenzer, A., Peters, M., Petry, T. and Clauss, T. 2022. Regional entrepreneurial ecosystems: how family firm embeddedness triggers ecosystem development. *Review of Managerial Science* 16, 15–44.

Bienkowska, D. and Klofsten, M. 2012. Creating entrepreneurial networks: academic entrepreneurship, mobility and collaboration during PhD education. *Higher Education* 64, 207–222.

Binz, C., Truffer, B. and Coenen, L. 2014. Why space matters in technological innovations systems – mapping global knowledge dynamics of membrane bioreactor technology. *Research Policy* 43(1), 138–155.

Boh, W. F., De-Haan, U. and Strom, R. 2016. University technology transfer through entrepreneurship: faculty and students in spinoffs. *Journal of Technology Transfer* 41, 661–669.

Bolzani, D., Fini, R., Grimaldi, R., Santoni, S. and Sobrero, M. 2014. Fifteen years of academic entrepreneurship in Italy: Evidence from the TASTE Project. University of Bologna, Italy.

Bonardo, D. Paleari, S. and Vismara, S. 2011. Valuing university-based firms: the effects of academic affiliation on IPO performance. *Entrepreneurship Theory and Practice* 35(4), 755–776.

Bourelos, E., Magnusson, M. and McKelvey, M. 2012. Investigating the complexity facing academic entrepreneurs in science and engineering: the complementarities of research performance, networks and support structures in commercialisation. *Cambridge Journal of Economics* 36(3), 751–780.

Bradley, S. R., Hayter, C. S. and Link, A. N. 2013. Proof of concept centers in the United States: an exploratory look. *Journal of Technology Transfer* 38, 349–381.

Bramwell, A. and Wolfe, D. A. 2008. Universities and regional economic development: the entrepreneurial University of Waterloo. *Research Policy* 37(8), 1175–1187.

Braunerhjelm, P. 2007. Academic entrepreneurship: social norms, university culture and policies. *Science and Public Policy* 34(9), 619–631.

Breznitz, S. M. and Zhang, Q. 2019. Fostering the growth of student start-ups from university accelerators: an entrepreneurial ecosystem perspective. *Industrial and Corporate Change* 28(4), 855–873.

Brooksbank, D. and Thomas, B. 2001. An assessment of higher education spin-off enterprises in Wales. *Industry & Higher Education* 15(6), 415–420.

Brouwer, A., Mariotti, I. and van Ommeren, J. 2004. The firm relocation decision: an empirical investigation. *Annals of Regional Science* 38, 335–347.

Brown, R. 2016. Mission impossible? Entrepreneurial universities and peripheral regional innovation systems. *Industry and Innovation* 23(2), 189–205.

Brown, R. and Mason, C. 2017. Looking inside the spiky bits: a critical review and conceptualisation of entrepreneurial ecosystems. *Small Business Economics* 49, 11–30.

Burt, R. S. 1992. *Structural Holes: The Social Structure of Competition.* Harvard University Press, London.

BVCA. 2022. BVCA Report on Investment Activity 2021. British Venture Capital Association, London, UK.

BVCA/Library House. 2005. Creating Success from University Spin-outs. British Venture Capital Association, London.

Caiazza, R., Belitski, M. and Audretsch, D. B. 2020. From latent to emergent entrepreneurship: the knowledge spillover construction circle. *Journal of Technology Transfer* 45, 694–704.

Cantner, U., Cunningham, J. A., Lehman, E. E. and Menter, M. 2021. Entrepreneurial ecosystems: a dynamic lifecycle model. *Small Business Economics* 57, 407–423.

Carayannis, E. G. and von Zedtwitz, M. 2005. Architecting gloCal (global–local), real–virtual incubator networks (G-RVINs) as catalysts and accelerators of entrepreneurship in transitioning and developing economies: lessons learned and best practices from current development and business incubation practices. *Technovation* 25(2), 95–110.

Carlsson, B., Acs, Z. J., Audretsch, D. B. and Braunerhjelm, P. 2007. The knowledge filter, entrepreneurship, and economic growth. Jena Economic Research Paper no. 2007-057, GMU School of Public Policy Research Paper no. 2010-12.

Carrincazeaux, C. and Coris, M. 2015. Why do firms relocate? Lessons from a regional analysis. *European Planning Studies* 23(9), 1695–1721.

Charles. D. 2016. The rural university campus and support for rural innovation. *Science and Public Policy* 43(6), 763–773.

Civera, A., De Massis, A., Meoli, M. and Vismara, S. 2024. The goal and performance heterogeneity of academic spinoffs. *Technovation* 131, 102972.

Clarysse, B., Wright, M., Lockett, A., Van de Velde, E. and Vohora, A. 2005. Spinning out new ventures: a typology of incubation strategies from European research institutions. *Journal of Business Venturing* 20(2), 183–216.

Clarysse, B., Wright, M., Lockett, A., Mustar, P. and Knockaert, M. 2007. Academic spin-offs, formal technology transfer and capital raising. *Industrial and Corporate Change* 16(4), 609–640.

Clarysse, B., Tartari, V. and Salter, A. 2011. The impact of entrepreneurial capacity, experience and organizational support on academic entrepreneurship. *Research Policy* 40(8), 1084–1093.

Clarysse, B., Wright, M. and Van de Velde, E. 2011. Entrepreneurial origin, technological knowledge, and the growth of spin-off companies. *Journal of Management Studies* 48(6), 1420–1442.

Clifton, N., Huggin, R., Pickernell, D., Prokop, D., Smith, D. and Thompson, P. 2020. Networking and strategic planning to enhance small and medium-sized enterprises in a less competitive economy. *Strategic Change* 29(6), 699–711.

Cloutier, L. and Messeghem, K. 2022. Whirlwind model of entrepreneurial ecosystem path dependence. *Small Business Economics* 59, 611–625.

Cohen, B. 2006. Sustainable valley entrepreneurial ecosystems. *Business Strategy and the Environment* 15(1), 1–14.

Cohen, W. M. and Levinthal, D. A. 1990. Absorptive capacity: a new perspective on learning and innovation. *Administrative Science Quarterly* 35(1), 128–152.

Collins, C. S. 2012. Land-grant extension as a global endeavour: connecting knowledge and international development. *The Review of Higher Education* 36(1), 91–124.

Colombelli, A., Paolucci, E. and Ughetto, E. 2019. Hierarchical and relational governance and the life cycle of entrepreneurial ecosystems. *Small Business Economics* 52, 505–521.

Compagnucci, L. and Spigarelli, F. 2020. The Third Mission of the university: a systematic literature review on potentials and constraints. *Technological Forecasting & Social Change* 161, 120284.

Cooke, P. 1992. Regional innovation systems: competitive regulation in the new Europe. *Geoforum* 23(3), 365–382.

Crespo, J., Suire, R. and Vicente, J. 2014. Lock-in or lock-out? How structural properties of knowledge networks affect regional resilience. *Journal of Economic Geography* 14(1), 199–219.

Criaco, G., Minola, T., Migliorini, P. and Serarols-Tarrés, C. 2014. 'To have and have not': founders' human capital and university start-up survival. *Journal of Technology Transfer* 39, 567–593.

Cukier, D., Kon, F. and Krueger, N. (2015). Designing a maturity model for software startup ecosystems. 16th International Conference PROFES 2015, Bolzano, Italy.

Czarnitzki, D., Rammer, C. and Toole, A. A. 2014. University spin-offs and the 'performance premium'. *Small Business Economics* 43, 309–326.

Davis, D. R. and Weinstein, D. E. 1999. Economic geography and regional production structure: an empirical investigation. *European Economic Review* 43(2), 379–407.

De Prijcker, S., Manigart, S., Collewaert, V. and Vanacker, T. 2019. Relocation to get venture capital: a resource dependence perspective. *Entrepreneurship Theory & Practice* 43(4), 697–724.

De Turi, I. and Antonicelli, M. 2019. Can the external environment generate better economic performance in academic spin-offs? *International Business Review* 12(11), 30–37.

DEFRA. 2021. Rural Urban Classification. Available online at: https://www.gov.uk/government/collections/rural-urban-classification [Accessed on 05/01/2023].

Degroof, J.-J. and Roberts, E. B. 2004. Overcoming weak entrepreneurial infrastructures for academic spin-off ventures. *Journal of Technology Transfer* 29(3–4), 327–352.

D'Este, P., Mahdi, S., Neely, A. and Rentocchini, F. 2012. Inventors and entrepreneurs in academia: what types of skills and experience matter? *Technovation* 32(5), 293–303.

Di Gregorio, D. and Shane, S. 2003. Why do some universities generate more start-ups than others? *Research Policy* 32, 209–227.

Doutriaux, J. 1987. Growth pattern of academic entrepreneurial firms. *Journal of Business Venturing* 2, 285–297.

Drucker, J. and Goldstein, H. 2007. Assessing the regional economic development impacts of universities: a review of current approaches. *International Regional Science Review* 30(1), 20–46.

Epure, M., Prior, D. and Serarols, C. 2016. Assessing technology-based spin-offs from university support units. *Regional Studies* 50(3), 411–428.

ETH Zürich. 2024. Overview of the entrepreneurship ecosystem – inside and outside ETH Zurich. Available at: https://ethz.ch/en/industry/entrepreneurship/discover-entrepreneurship-ecosystem.html [Accessed on 23/01/2024].

Etzkowitz, H. and Leydesdorff, L. 1995. The triple helix university–industry–government relations: a laboratory for knowledge based economic development. *EASTT Review* 14, 14–19.

Etzkowitz, H. and Leydesdorff, L. 2000. The dynamics of innovation: from National Systems and 'Mode 2' to a triple helix of university–industry–government relations. *Research Policy* 29, 109–123.

Feldman, M. P. and Zoller, T. D. 2016. Dealmakers in place: social capital connections in regional entrepreneurial economies. In Westlund, H. and Larsson, J. P. (eds). *Handbook of Social Capital and Regional Development*. Edward Elgar Publishing, Cheltenham, UK and Northampton, MA, USA, pp. 141–165.

Fini, R., Grimaldi, R. and Sobrero, M. 2009. Factors fostering academics to start up new ventures: an assessment of Italian founders' incentives. *Journal of Technology Transfer* 34, 380–402.

Fini, R., Lacetera, N. and Shane, S. 2010. Inside or outside the IP system? Business creation in academia. *Research Policy* 39(8), 1060–1069.

Fini, R., Grimaldi, R., Santoni, S. and Sobrero, M. 2011. Complements or substitutes? The role of universities and local context in supporting the creation of academic spin-offs. *Research Policy* 40(8), 1113–1127.

Fini, R., Fu, K., Mathisen, M. T., Rasmussen, E. and Wright, M. 2017. Institutional determinants of university spin-off quantity and quality: a longitudinal, multilevel, cross-country study. *Small Business Economics* 48(2), 361–391.

Fitzgerald, C. and Cunningham, J. 2016. Inside the university technology transfer office: mission statement analysis. *Journal of Technology Transfer* 41(5), 1235–1246.

FLC. 2018. *Federal Technology Transfer Legislation and Policy: The Green Book*. Federal Laboratory Consortium for Technology Transfer, US.

Florida, R. 1995. Toward the learning region. *Futures* 27(5), 527–536.

Foccaci, C. N. and Kirov, V. 2021. Regional entrepreneurial ecosystems: technological transformation, digitalisation and the longer term – the automotive and ICT sectors in the UK and Bulgaria. *Local Economy* 36(1), 56–74.

Forslid, R. and Okubo, T. 2014. Spatial sorting with heterogeneous firms and heterogeneous sectors. *Regional Science and Urban Economics* 46, 42–56.

Franklin, S. J., Wright, M. and Lockett, A. 2001. Academic and surrogate entrepreneurs in university spin-out companies. *Journal of Technology Transfer* 26, 127–141.

Frimanslund, T. 2022. Financial entrepreneurial ecosystems: an analysis of urban and rural regions of Norway. *International Journal of Global Business and Competitiveness* 17, 24–39.

Gallup, J. L., Sachs, J. D. and Mellinger, A. D. 1999. Geography and economic development. *International Regional Science Review* 22(2), 179–232.

Garnsey, E. and Heffernan, P. 2005. High-technology clustering through spin-out and attraction: the Cambridge case. *Regional Studies* 39(8), 1127–1144.

Gaubert, C. 2018. Firm sorting and agglomeration. *American Economic Review* 108(11), 3117–3153.

Geroski, P. A. 1995. What do we know about entry? *International Journal of Industrial Organization* 13, 421–440.

Ghio, N., Guerini, M., Lehmann, E. E. and Rossi-Lamastra, C. 2015. The emergence of the knowledge spillover theory of entrepreneurship. *Small Business Economics* 44, 1–18.

Gilsing, V. A., van Burg, E. and Romme, A. G. L. 2010. Policy principles for the creation and success of corporate and academic spin-offs. *Technovation* 30(1), 12–23.

Godley, A., Morawetz, N. and Soga, L. 2021. The complementarity perspective to the entrepreneurial ecosystem taxonomy. *Small Business Economics* 56, 723–738.

Goethner, M., Obschonka, M., Silbereisen, R. K. and Cantner, U. 2012. Scientists' transition to academic entrepreneurship: economic and psychological determinants. *Journal of Economic Psychology* 33(3), 628–641.

Goldstein, H. and Renault, C. 2004. Contributions of universities to regional economic development: a quasi-experimental approach. *Regional Studies* 38, 733–746.

Gonzalez-Pernia, J. L., Kuechle, G. and Peña-Legazkue, I. 2013. An assessment of the determinants of university technology transfer. *Economic Development Quarterly* 27(1), 6–17.

Good, M., Knockaert, M., Soppe, B. and Wright, M. 2019. The technology transfer ecosystem in academia: an organizational design perspective. *Technovation* 82–83, 35–50.

Grandi, A. and Grimaldi, R. 2003. Exploring the networking characteristics of new venture founding teams. *Small Business Economics* 21(4), 329–341.

Granovetter, M. S. 1973. The strength of weak ties. *American Journal of Sociology* 78(6), 1360–1380.

Gregory, R., Lombard, J. R. and Seifert, B. 2005. Impact of headquarters relocation on the operating performance of the firm. *Economic Development Quarterly* 19(3), 260–270.

Grimaldi, R. and Grandi, A. 2005. Business incubators and new venture creation: an assessment of incubating models. *Technovation* 25(2), 111–121.

Grimaldi, R., Kenney, M., Siegel, D. S. and Wright, M. 2011. 30 years after Bayh–Dole: reassessing academic entrepreneurship. *Research Policy* 40(8), 1045–1057.

Gubitta, P., Tognazzo, A. and Destro, F. 2016. Signalling in academic ventures: the role of technology transfer offices and university funds. *Journal of Technology Transfer* 41, 368–393.

Gueguen, G., Delanoë-Gueguen, S. and Lechner, C. 2021. Start-ups in entrepreneurial ecosystems: the role of relational capacity. *Management Decision* 59(13), 115–135.

Guerrero, M. and Urbano, D. 2014. Academics' start-up intentions and knowledge filters: an individual perspective of the knowledge spillover theory of entrepreneurship. *Small Business Economics* 43, 57–74.

Haarhaus, T., Strunk, G. and Liening, A. 2020. Assessing the complex dynamics of entrepreneurial ecosystems: a nonstationary approach. *Journal of Business Venturing Insights* 14, e00194.

Haeussler, C. and Colyvas, J. A. 2011. Breaking the ivory tower: academic entrepreneurship in the life sciences in UK and Germany. *Research Policy* 40(1), 41–54.

Hallam, C., De La Vina, L., Leffel, A. and Agrawal, M. 2014. Accelerating collegiate entrepreneurship (ACE): the architecture of a university entrepreneurial ecosystem encompassing an intercollegiate venture experience. *Journal of Business and Entrepreneurship* 26(2), 95–116.

Hallam, C., Novick, D., Gilbert, D. J., Frankwick, G. L., Wenker, O. and Zanella, G. 2017. Academic entrepreneurship and the entrepreneurial ecosystem: the UT Transform Project. *Academy of Entrepreneurship Journal* 23(1), 77–90.

Harmon, B., Ardishvili, A., Cardozo, R., Elder, T., Leuthold, J., Parshall, J., Raghian, M. and Smith, D. 1997. Mapping the university technology transfer process. *Journal of Business Venturing* 12, 423–434.

Harrison, R. T. and Leitch, C. 2010. Voodoo institution or entrepreneurial university? Spin-off companies, the entrepreneurial system and regional development in the UK. *Regional Studies* 44(9), 1241–1262.

Hayter, C. S. 2011. In search of the profit-maximizing actor: motivations and definitions of success from nascent academic entrepreneurs. *Journal of Technology Transfer* 36(3), 340–352.

Hayter, C. S. 2013. Harnessing university entrepreneurship for economic growth: factors of success among university spin-offs. *Economic Development Quarterly* 27(1), 18–28.

Hayter, C. S. 2016. Constraining entrepreneurial development: a knowledge-based view of social networks among academic entrepreneurs. *Research Policy* 45, 475–490.

Hayter, C. S., Lubynsky, R. and Maroulis, S. 2017. Who is the academic entrepreneur? The role of graduate students in the development of university spinoffs. *Journal of Technology Transfer* 42, 1237–1254.

Hayter, C. S., Nelson, A. J., Zayed, S. and O'Connor, A. C. 2018. Conceptualizing academic entrepreneurship ecosystems: a review, analysis and extension of the literature. *Journal of Technology Transfer* 43, 1039–1082.

Heaton, S., Siegel, D. S. and Teece, D. J. 2019. Universities and innovation ecosystems: a dynamic capabilities perspective. *Industrial and Corporate Change* 28(4), 921–939.

Heblich, S. and Slavtchev, V. 2014. Parent universities and the location decision of academic startups. *Small Business Economics* 42, 1–15.

Henard, D. H. and McFadyen, M. A. 2005. The complementary roles of applied and basic research: a knowledge-based perspective. *Journal of Product Innovation Management* 22(6), 503–514.

Hewitt-Dundas, N. 2012. Research intensity and knowledge transfer activity in UK universities. *Research Policy* 41, 262–275.

Hewitt-Dundas, N. 2015. Profiling UK university spin-outs. ERC Research Paper No. 35. Enterprise Research Centre.

Holgersson, M. and Aaboen, L. 2019. A literature review of intellectual property management in technology transfer offices: from appropriation to utilization. *Technology in Society* 59, 101132.

Hossinger, S. M., Chen, X. and Werner, A. 2020. Drivers, barriers and success factors of academic spin-offs: a systematic literature review. *Management Review Quarterly* 70, 97–134.

Howells, J. 2005. Innovation and regional economic development: a matter of perspective? *Research Policy* 34(8), 1220–1234.

Huang-Saad, A., Fay, J. and Sheridan, L. 2017. Closing the divide: accelerating technology commercialization by catalyzing the university entrepreneurial ecosystem with I-Corps™. *Journal of Technology Transfer* 42, 1466–1486.

Huggins, R. 2008. The evolution of knowledge clusters: progress and policy. *Economic Development Quarterly* 22(4), 277–289.

Huggins, R. 2010. Forms of network resource: knowledge access and the role of inter-firm networks. *International Journal of Management Reviews* 12(3), 335–352.

Huggins, R. and Prokop, D. 2014. Stock markets and economic development: the case for regional exchanges. *International Journal of Innovation and Regional Development* 5(3), 279–303.

Huggins, R. and Prokop, D. 2017. Network structure and regional innovation: a study of university–industry ties. *Urban Studies* 54(4), 931–952.

Huggins, R. and Thompson, P. 2015. Culture and place-based development: a socio-economic analysis. *Regional Studies* 49(1), 130–159.

Huggins, R., Izushi, H., Clifton, N., Jenkins, S., Prokop, D. and Whitfield, C. 2010. Sourcing knowledge for innovation: the international dimension. NESTA, London.

Huggins, R., Izushi, H., Prokop, D. and Thompson, P. 2014. *The Global Competitiveness of Regions*. Routledge, London.

Huggins, R., Prokop, D., Steffenson, R., Johnston, A. and Clifton, N. 2014. The engagement of entrepreneurial firms with universities: network formation, innovation and resilience. *Journal of General Management* 40(1), 23–51.

Huggins, R., Izushi, H. and Prokop, D. 2016. Networks, space and organizational performance: a study of the determinants of industrial research income generation by universities. *Regional Studies* 50(12), 2055–2068.

Huggins, R., Prokop, D. and Thompson, P. 2017. Entrepreneurship and the determinants of firm survival within regions: human capital, growth motivation and locational conditions. *Entrepreneurship & Regional Development* 29(3–4), 357–389.

Huggins, R., Izushi, H. and Prokop, D. 2019. Regional advantage and the geography of networks: explaining global–local knowledge sourcing patterns. *Papers in Regional Science* 98(4), 1567–1584.

Huggins, R., Prokop, D. and Thompson, P. 2020. Universities and open innovation: the determinants of network centrality. *Journal of Technology Transfer* 45, 718–757.

Huggins, R., Prokop, D. and Thompson, P. 2021. UK Competitiveness Index 2021. Cardiff and Nottingham Trent Universities.

Huggins, R., Kitagawa, F., Prokop, D., Theodoraki, C. and Thompson, P. 2024. *Entrepreneurial Ecosystems in Cities and Regions: Emergence, Evolution, and Future.* Oxford University Press, Oxford.

Iacobucci, D. 1994. Graphs and matrices. In Wasserman, S. and Faust, K. (eds). *Social Network Analysis: Methods and Applications.* Structural Analysis in the Social Sciences. Cambridge University Press, Cambridge, pp. 92–166.

Iftikhar, M. N., Ahmad, M. and Audretsch, D. B. 2020. The knowledge spillover theory of entrepreneurship: the developing country context. *International Entrepreneurial Management Journal* 16, 1327–1346.

Isenberg, D. (2011). The entrepreneurship ecosystem strategy as a new paradigm for economic policy: principles for cultivating entrepreneurship. Dublin: Institute of International European Affairs.

Jain, S. and George, G. 2007. Technology transfer offices as institutional entrepreneurs: the case of Wisconsin Alumni Research Foundation and human embryonic stem cells. *Industrial and Corporate Change* 16(4), 535–567.

Jensen, R. A., Thursby, J. G. and Thursby, M. C. 2003. Disclosure and licensing of university inventions: 'The best we can do with the s**t we get to work with'. *International Journal of Industrial Organization* 21(9), 1271–1300.

Johnston, A. and Prokop, D. 2021. Peripherality and university collaboration: evidence from rural SMEs in the UK. *Journal of Rural Studies* 88, 298–306.

Kapitsinis, N. 2017. Firm relocation in times of economic crisis: evidence from Greek small and medium enterprises' movement to Bulgaria, 2007–2014. *European Planning Studies* 25(4), 703–725.

Kapturkiewicz, A. 2022. Varieties of Entrepreneurial Ecosystems: a comparative study of Tokyo and Bangalore. *Research Policy* 51, 104377.

Kenney, M. and Patton, D. 2009. Reconsidering the Bayh–Dole Act and the current university invention ownership model. *Research Policy* 38(9), 1407–1422.

Kitagawa, F., Marzocchi, C., Sanchez-Barrioluengo, M. and Uyarra, E. 2022. Anchoring talent to regions: the role of universities in graduate retention through employment and entrepreneurship. *Regional Studies* 56(6), 1001–1014.

Klagge, B. and Martin, R. 2005. Decentralized versus centralized financial systems: is there a case for local capital markets? *Journal of Economic Geography* 5(4), 387–421.

Knie, A. and Lengwiler, M. 2008. Token endeavors: the significance of academic spin-offs in technology transfer and research policy in Germany. *Science and Public Policy* 35(3), 171–182.

Knoben, J. and Oerlemans, L. 2005. The effects of firm relocation on firm performance – a literature review. 45th Congress of the European Regional Science Association: 'Land Use and Water Management in a Sustainable Network Society', 23–27 August 2005, Amsterdam, the Netherlands.

Koroleva E. 2022. FinTech entrepreneurial ecosystems: exploring the interplay between input and output. *International Journal of Financial Studies* 10(4), 1–19.

Krabel, S. and Mueller, P. 2009. What drives scientists to start their own company? *Research Policy* 38(6), 947–956.

Krabel, S., Siegel, D. S. and Slavtchev, V. 2012. The internationalization of science and its influence on academic entrepreneurship. *Journal of Technology Transfer* 37, 192–212.

Kreutzer, F. and Mitze, T. 2017. Going offshore or better staying in? Spatial relocation strategies and their impact on firm innovativeness. *Applied Economics Letters* 24(12), 837–840.

Kronenberg, K. 2013. Firm relocations in the Netherlands: why do firms move, and where do they go? *Papers in Regional Science* 92(4), 691–713.

Krugman, P. 1999. The role of geography in development. *International Regional Science Review* 22(2), 142–161.

Lafuente, E., Szerb, L. and Ács, Z. J. 2023. The entrepreneurship paradox: the role of the entrepreneurial ecosystem on economic performance in Africa. In Acs, Z. J., Lafuente, E. and Szerb, L. (eds). *The Entrepreneurial Ecosystem*. Palgrave Studies in Entrepreneurship and Society. Palgrave Macmillan, Cham, pp. 103–146.

Lahikainen, K., Kolhinen, J., Ruskovaara, E. and Pihkala, T. 2019. Challenges to the development of an entrepreneurial university ecosystem: the case of a Finnish university campus. *Industry and Higher Education* 33(2), 96–107.

Lam, A. 2011. What motivates academic scientists to engage in research commercialization: 'gold', 'ribbon' or 'puzzle'? *Research Policy* 40(10), 1354–1368.

Lambert, R. 2003. *Lambert Review of Business University Collaboration*. HMSO, Norwich.

Landry, R., Amara, N. and Rherrad, I. 2006. Why are some university researchers more likely to create spin-offs than others? Evidence from Canadian universities. *Research Policy* 35(10), 1599–1615.

Lawton-Smith, H. and Ho, K. 2006. Measuring the performance of Oxford University, Oxford Brookes University and the government laboratories' spin-off companies. *Research Policy* 35(10), 1554–1568.

Lawton-Smith, H., Romeo, S. and Bagchi-Sen, S. 2008. Oxfordshire biomedical university spin-offs: an evolving system. *Cambridge Journal of Regions, Economy and Society* 1(2), 303–319.

Lawton-Smith, H., Chapman, D., Wood, P., Barnes, T. and Romeo, S. 2014. Entrepreneurial academics and regional innovation systems: the case of spin-offs from London's universities. *Environment and Planning C: Government and Policy* 32, 341–359.

Lee, I. H. 2022. Startups, relocation, and firm performance: a transaction cost economics perspective. *Small Business Economics* 58, 205–224.

Lehrer, M. and Asakawa, K. 2004. Pushing scientists into the marketplace: promoting science entrepreneurship. *California Management Review* 46(3), 55–76.

Link, A. N. and Sarala, R. M. 2019. Advancing conceptualisation of university entrepreneurial ecosystems: the role of knowledge-intensive entrepreneurial firms. *International Small Business Journal* 37(3), 289–310.

Lockett, A. and Wright, M. 2005. Resources, capabilities, risk capital and the creation of university spin-out companies. *Research Policy* 34(7), 1043–1057.

Lockett, A., Wright, M. and Franklin, S. 2003. Technology transfer and universities' spin-out strategies. *Small Business Economics* 20, 185–200.

Lundvall, B.-Å. 1992. *National Systems of Innovation: Towards a Theory of Innovation and Interactive Learning*. Pinter, London.

Macho-Stadler, I., Pérez-Castrillo, D. and Veugelers, R. 2007. Licensing of university inventions: the role of a technology transfer office. *International Journal of Industrial Organization* 25(3), 483–510.

Mack, E. and Mayer, H. 2016. The evolutionary dynamics of entrepreneurial ecosystems. *Urban Studies* 53(10), 2118–2133.

Maggioni, M. A. and Uberti, T. E. 2011. Networks and geography in the economics of knowledge flows. *Quality and Quantity* 45, 1031–1051.

Malecki, E. J. 2018. Entrepreneurship and entrepreneurial ecosystems. *Geography Compass* 12(3), 1–21.

Mariotti, I. 2005. Firm relocation and regional policy: a focus on Italy, the Netherlands and the United Kingdom. Thesis at University of Groningen.

Markman, G. D., Phan, P. H., Balkin, D. B. and Gianiodis, P. T. 2005. Entrepreneurship and university-based technology transfer. *Journal of Business Venturing* 20(2), 241–263.

Marzocchi, C., Kitagawa, F. and Sanchez-Barrioluengo, M. 2019. Evolving missions and university entrepreneurship: academic spin-offs and graduate start-ups in the entrepreneurial society. *Journal of Technology Transfer* 44, 167–188.

Mason, C. and Brown, R. 2014. Entrepreneurial ecosystems and growth oriented entrepreneurship. Background paper. OECD, The Hague.

Mason, C. M. and Harrison, R. T. 2006. After the exit: acquisitions, entrepreneurial recycling and regional economic development. *Regional Studies* 40(1), 55–73.

Miller, D. J. and Acs, Z. J. 2017. The campus as entrepreneurial ecosystem: the University of Chicago. *Small Business Economics* 49, 75–95.

Morgan, K. 1997. The learning region: institutions, innovation and regional renewal. *Regional Studies* 31(5), 491–503.

Motoyama, Y. and Mayer, H. 2017. Revisiting the roles of the university in regional economic development: a triangulation of data. *Growth and Change* 48(4), 787–804.

Mueller, P. 2006. Exploring the knowledge filter: how entrepreneurship and university–industry relationships drive economic growth. *Research Policy* 35(10), 1499–1508.

Muñoz, P., Kibler, E., Mandakovic, V. and Amorós, J. E. 2022. Local entrepreneurial ecosystems as configural narratives: a new way of seeing and evaluating antecedents and outcomes. *Research Policy* 51, 104065.

Naz, A., Niebuhr, A. and Peters, J. C. 2015. What's behind the disparities in firm innovation rates across regions? Evidence on composition and context effects. *Annals of Regional Science* 55, 131–156.

Ndonzuau, F. N., Pirnay, F. and Surlemont, B. 2002. A stage model of academic spin-off creation. *Technovation* 22(5), 281–289.

Nerkar, A. and Shane, S. 2003. When do start-ups that exploit patented academic knowledge survive? *International Journal of Industrial Organization* 21, 1391–1410.

Niebuhr, A., Peters, J. C. and Schmidke, A. 2020. Spatial sorting of innovative firms and heterogeneous effects of agglomeration on innovation in Germany. *Journal of Technology Transfer* 45, 1343–1375.

Nkusi, A. C., Cunningham, J. A., Nyuur, R. and Pattinson, S. 2020. The role of the entrepreneurial university in building an entrepreneurial ecosystem in a post conflict economy: an exploratory study of Rwanda. *Thunderbird: International Business Review* 62, 549–563.

Nonaka, I. 1991. The knowledge-creating company. *Harvard Business Review* November–December, 162–171.

Nonaka, I. 1994. A dynamic theory of organizational knowledge creation. *Organization Science* 5(1), 14–37.

Nordling, N. 2019. Public policy's role and capability in fostering the emergence and evolution of entrepreneurial ecosystems: a case of ecosystem-based policy in Finland. *Local Economy* 34(8), 807–824.

OECD/EU. 2019. Supporting Entrepreneurship and Innovation in Higher Education in Italy. OECD Skills Studies, OECD Publishing, Paris. Available at: https://doi.org/10.1787/43e88f48-en.

ONS. 2022. Business demography, UK: 2021. Office for National Statistics. Available at: https://www.ons.gov.uk/businessindustryandtrade/business/activitysizeandlocation/bulletins/businessdemography/2021#:~:text=Between%202020%20and%202021%2C%20the,compared%20with%2011.5%25%20in%202020 [Accessed on 24/01/2023].

Ortín-Ángel, P. and Vendrell-Herrero, F. 2010. Why do university spin-offs attract more venture capitalists? *Venture Capital* 12(4), 285–306.

Ortín-Ángel, P. and Vendrell-Herrero, F. 2014. University spin-offs vs. other NTBFs: total factor productivity differences at outset and evolution. *Technovation* 34, p. 101–112.

O'Shea, R. P., Allen, T. J., Chevalier, A. and Roche, F. 2005. Entrepreneurial orientation, technology transfer and spinoff performance of U.S. universities. *Research Policy* 34(7), 994–1009.

Padilla-Meléndez, A., Fuster, E., Lockett, N. and del-Aguila-Obra, A. R. 2021. Knowledge spillovers, knowledge filters and entrepreneurial university ecosystems: emerging role of university-focused venture capital firms. *Knowledge Management Research & Practice* 19(1), 94–105.

Parker, S. C. 2009. Can cognitive biases explain venture team homophily? *Strategic Entrepreneurship Journal* 3, 67–83.

Parmentola, A. and Ferretti, M. 2018. Stages and trigger factors in the development of academic spin-offs: an explorative study in southern Italy. *European Journal of Innovation Management* 21(3), 478–500.

Pellenbarg, P. H., van Wissen, L. J. G. and van Dijk, J. 2002. Firm relocation: state of the art and research prospects. University of Groningen, SOM research school, 1–42.

Pennings, E. and Sleuwaegen, L. 2000. International relocation: firm and industry determinants. *Economics Letters* 67(2), 179–186.

Pike, A., Marlow, A., O'Brien, P. and Tomaney, J. 2015. Local institutions and local economic development: the Local Enterprise Partnerships in England, 2010–. *Cambridge Journal of Regions, Economy and Society* 8(2), 185–204.

Pita, M., Costa, J. and Moreira, A. C. 2021. Entrepreneurial ecosystems and entrepreneurial initiative: building a multi-country taxonomy. *Sustainability* 13, 1–26.

Plummer, L. A. and Pe'er, A. 2010. The geography of entrepreneurship. In Acs, Z. and Audretsch, D. (eds). *Handbook of Entrepreneurship Research.* International Handbook Series on Entrepreneurship, vol. 5. Springer, New York, pp. 519–556.

Porter, M. 1990. *The Competitive Advantage of Nations.* Macmillan, Basingstoke.

Prodan, I. and Drnovsek, M. 2010. Conceptualizing academic–entrepreneurial intentions: an empirical test. *Technovation* 30(5–6), 332–347.

Prokop, D. 2017. The determinants of university spinout formation and survival: the UK context of network, investment, and management team effects. PhD Thesis, Cardiff University.

Prokop, D. 2021. University entrepreneurial ecosystems and spinoff companies: configurations, developments and outcomes. *Technovation* 107, 102286. Doi:10.1016/j.technovation.2021.102286.

Prokop, D. 2022. The composition of university entrepreneurial ecosystems and academic entrepreneurship: a UK study. *International Journal of Innovation and Technology Management* 19(6), 1–23.

Prokop, D. 2023. The academic spinoff theory of the firm. *The International Journal of Entrepreneurship and Innovation* 24(4) 233–243.

Prokop, D. and Kitagawa, F. 2022. Shareholder networks of university spinoff companies: firm development and regional characteristics. *Studies in Higher Education* 47(10), 2101–2116.

Prokop, D. and Thompson, P. 2023. Defining networks in entrepreneurial ecosystems: the openness of ecosystems. *Small Business Economics* 61(2), 517–538.

Prokop, D., Huggins, R. and Bristow, G. 2019. The survival of academic spinoff companies: an empirical study of key determinants. *International Small Business Journal* 37(5), 502–535.

Prokop, D., Tabari, S. and Chen, W. 2024. Survival instincts of Chinese entrepreneurs in the UK: adaptation or hibernation. *International Journal of Entrepreneurship and Small Business*, DOI: 10.1504/IJESB.2025.10059695.

Qian, H. and Jung, H. 2017. Solving the knowledge filter puzzle: absorptive capacity, entrepreneurship and regional development. *Small Business Economics* 48, 99–114.

Rasmussen, E. 2011. Understanding academic entrepreneurship: exploring the emergence of university spin-off ventures using process theories. *International Small Business Journal* 29(5), 448–471.

Rasmussen, E. and Wright, M. 2015. How can universities facilitate academic spin-offs? An entrepreneurial competency perspective. *Journal of Technology Transfer* 40, 782–799.

Rasmussen, E., Mosey, S. and Wright, M. 2015. The transformation of network ties to develop entrepreneurial competencies for university spin-offs. *Entrepreneurship & Regional Development* 27(7–8), 430–457.

Ratten, V. and Thompson, A.-J. 2020. Digital sport entrepreneurial ecosystems. *Thunderbird: International Business Review* 62, 565–578.

Rocha, A., Brown, R. and Mawson, S. 2021. Capturing conversations in entrepreneurial ecosystems. *Research Policy* 50, 104317.

Rodríguez-Pose, A. 2013. Do institutions matter for regional development? *Regional Studies* 47(7), 1034–1047.

Rodríguez-Pose, A. 2020. Institutions and the fortunes of territories. *Regional Science Policy & Practice* 12(3), 371–386.

Romer, P. M. 1990. Endogenous technological change. *Journal of Political Economy*, 98, 71–102.

Rossi, F. and Dej, M. 2020. Where do firms relocate? Location optimisation within and between Polish metropolitan areas. *Annals of Regional Science* 64, 615–640.

Roundy, P. T. 2016. Start-up community narratives: the discursive construction of entrepreneurial ecosystems. *Journal of Entrepreneurship and Innovation in Emerging Economies* 25(2), 232–248.

Roundy, P. T. 2017. The resilience of entrepreneurial ecosystems. *Journal of Business Venturing Insights* 8, 99–104.

Roundy, P. T., Bradshaw, M. and Brockman, B. K. 2018. The emergence of entrepreneurial ecosystems: a complex adaptive systems approach. *Journal of Business Research* 86, 1–10.

Ryan, P., Giblin, M., Buciuni, G. and Kogler, D. F. 2021. The role of MNEs in the genesis and growth of a resilient entrepreneurial ecosystem. *Entrepreneurship & Regional Development* 33(1–2), 36–53.

Salomaa, M., Charles, D. and Bosworth, G. 2022. Universities and innovation strategies in rural regions: the case of the greater Lincolnshire innovation programme (UK). *Industry and Higher Education* 37(1), 67–79.

Salvador, E. and Rolfo, S. 2011. Are incubators and science parks effective for research spin-offs? Evidence from Italy. *Science and Public Policy* 38(3), 170–184.

Sansone, G., Battaglia, D., Landoni, P. and Paolucci, E. 2021. Academic spinoffs: the role of entrepreneurship education. *International Entrepreneurship and Management Journal* 17, 369–399.

Sanström, C., Wennberg, K., Wallin, M. W. and Zherlygina, Y. 2018. Public policy for academic entrepreneurship initiatives: a review and critical discussion. *Journal of Technology Transfer* 43, 1232–1256.

Saxenian, A. 1994. *Regional Advantage: Culture and Competition in Silicon Valley and Route 128*. Harvard University Press, Cambridge, MA.

Schäfer, S. 2021. Spatialities of entrepreneurial ecosystems. *Geography Compass* 15, 1–10.

Schäfer, S. and Henn, S. 2018. The evolution of entrepreneurial ecosystems and the critical role of migrants: a phase-model based on a study of IT startups in the Greater Tel Aviv Area. *Cambridge Journal of Regions, Economy and Society* 11, 317–333.

Scholten, V., Omta, O., Kemp, R. and Elfring, T. 2015. Bridging ties and the role of research and start-up experience on the early growth of Dutch academic spin-offs. *Technovation* 45–46, 40–51.

Schutjens, V. and Völker, B. 2010. Space and social capital: the degree of locality in entrepreneurs' contacts and its consequences for firm success. *European Planning Studies* 18(6), 941–963.

Sciarelli, M., Landi, G. C., Turriziani, L. and Tani, M. 2021. Academic entrepreneurship: founding and governance determinants in university spin-off ventures. *Journal of Technology Transfer* 46, 1083–1107.

Scott, S., Hughes, M. and Ribeiro-Soriano, D. 2021. Towards a network-based view of effective entrepreneurial ecosystems. *Review of Managerial Science* 16, 157–187.

Secundo, G., Mele, G., Del Vecchio, P. and Degennaro, G. 2021. Knowledge spillover creation in university-based entrepreneurial ecosystem: the role of the Italian 'Contamination Labs'. *Knowledge Management Research & Practice* 19(1), 137–151.

Shane, S. 2004. *Academic Entrepreneurship. University Spinoffs and Wealth Creation*. Edward Elgar Publishing, Cheltenham, UK and Northampton, MA, USA.

Sharafizad, J. and Brown, K. 2020. Regional small business' personal and inter-firm networks. *Journal of Business & Industrial Marketing* 35(12), 1957–1969.

Shu, C., Gu, M., Liu, C. and Audretsch, D. B. 2022. The role of the government in the knowledge spillover theory of entrepreneurship: a firm-level analysis. *IEEE Transactions on Engineering Management* 69(5), 2311–2325.

Siegel, D. S., Waldman, D. A., Atwater, L. E. and Link, A. N. 2004. Toward a model of the effective transfer of scientific knowledge from academicians to practitioners: qualitative evidence from the commercialization of university technologies. *Journal of Engineering and Technology Management* 21(1–2), 115–142.

Siegel, D. S., Veugelers, R. and Wright, M. 2007. Technology transfer offices and commercialization of university intellectual property: performance and policy implications. *Oxford Review of Economic Policy* 23(4), 640–660.

Sim, L.-L., Ong, S.-E., Agarwal, A., Parsa, A. and Keivani, R. 2003. Singapore's competitiveness as a global city: development strategy, institutions and business environment. *Cities* 20(2), 115–127.

Slack, E. and Côté, A. 2014. Comparative urban governance. Future of cities: working paper. Foresight, Government Office for Science, London, UK.

Sousa-Ginel, E., Franco-Leal, N. and Camelo-Ordaz, C. 2017. The influence of networks on the knowledge conversion capability of academic spin-offs. *Industrial and Corporate Change* 26(6), 1125–1144.

Spigel, B. 2017. The relational organization of entrepreneurial ecosystems. *Entrepreneurship Theory & Practice* 41(1), 49–72.

Spigel, B. 2020. *Entrepreneurial Ecosystems: Theory, Practice, Futures.* Edward Elgar Publishing, Cheltenham, UK and Northampton, MA, USA.

Spigel, B. 2022. Examining the cohesiveness and nestedness entrepreneurial ecosystems: evidence from British FinTechs. *Small Business Economics* 59, 1381–1399.

Spigel, B. and Harrison, R. 2018. Toward a process theory of entrepreneurial ecosystems. *Strategic Entrepreneurship Journal* 12, 151–168.

Spigel, B. and Vinodrai, T. 2021. Meeting its Waterloo? Recycling in entrepreneurial ecosystems after anchor firm collapse. *Entrepreneurship & Regional Development* 33(7–8), 599–620.

Stam, E. 2015. Entrepreneurial ecosystems and regional policy: a sympathetic critique. *European Planning Studies* 23(9), 1759–1769.

Stam, E. and Van de Ven, A. 2021. Entrepreneurial ecosystem elements. *Small Business Economics* 56, 809–832.

Stanford University. 2024. Stanford Entrepreneurship Network. Available at: https://sen .stanford.edu/#:~:text=Stanford's%20entrepreneurial%20ecosystem%20is%20rich ,initiatives%20for%20the%20Stanford%20community [Accessed on 23/01/2024].

Sternberg, R. 2014. Success factors of university-spin-offs: regional government support programs versus regional environment. *Technovation* 34(3), 137–148.

Sternberg, R. 2022. Entrepreneurship and geography – some thoughts about a complex relationship. *Annals of Regional Science* 69, 559–584.

Storper, M. 1993. Regional 'worlds' of production: learning and innovation in the technology districts of France, Italy and the USA. *Regional Studies* 27(5), 433–455.

Sussan, F. and Acs, Z. J. 2017. The digital entrepreneurial ecosystem. *Small Business Economics* 49, 55–73.

Tamasy, C. 2007. Rethinking technology-oriented business incubators: developing a robust policy instrument for entrepreneurship, innovation, and regional development? *Growth and Change* 38(3), 460–473.

Ter Wal, A. L. J. and Boschma, R. A. 2009. Applying social network analysis in economic geography: framing some key analytic issues. *Annals of Regional Science* 43, 739–756.

Theodoraki, C. 2020. A holistic approach to incubator strategies in the entrepreneurial support ecosystem. *M@n@gement* 23(4), 13–27.

Theodoraki, C., Messeghem, K. and Rice, M. P. 2018. A social capital approach to the development of sustainable entrepreneurial ecosystems: an explorative study. *Small Business Economics* 51, 153–170.

Toole, A. A. and Czarnitzki, D. 2007. Biomedical academic entrepreneurship through the SBIR program. *Journal of Economic Behavior & Organization* 63(4), 716–738.

Toole, A. A. and Czarnitzki, D. 2010. Commercializing science: is there a university 'brain drain' from academic entrepreneurship? *Management Science* 56(9), 1599–1614.

Tracey, I. and Williamson, A. 2023. Independent review of spinout companies. Final report and recommendations. Department for Science, Innovation & Technology, UK.

Van Dijk, J. and Pellenbarg, P. 2000. Firm relocation decisions in The Netherlands: an ordered logit approach. *Papers in Regional Science* 79, 191–219.

Van Geenhuizen, M. and Soetanto, D. P. 2009. Academic spin-offs at different ages: a case study in search of key obstacles to growth. *Technovation* 29(10), 671–681.

Van Geenhuizen, M. and Soetanto, D. P. 2013. Benefitting from learning networks in 'open innovation': spin-off firms in contrasting city regions. *European Planning Studies* 21(5), 666–682.

Van Rijnsoever, F. J. 2020. Meeting, mating, and intermediating: how incubators can overcome weak network problems in entrepreneurial ecosystems. *Research Policy* 49, 103884.

Vedula, S. and Kim, P. H. 2019. Gimme shelter or fade away: the impact of regional entrepreneurial ecosystem quality on venture survival. *Industrial and Corporate Change* 28(4), 827–854.

Vincett P. S. 2010. The economic impacts of academic spin-off companies, and their implications for public policy. *Research Policy* 39, 736–747.

Visintin, F. and Pittino, D. 2014. Founding team composition and early performance of university-based spin-off companies. *Technovation* 34, 31–43.

Vohora, A., Wright, M. and Lockett, A. 2004. Critical junctures in the development of university high-tech spinout companies. *Research Policy* 33(1), 147–175.

Wadee, A. A. and Padayachee, A. 2017. Higher education: catalysts for the development of an entrepreneurial ecosystem, or … are we the weakest link? *Science, Technology & Society* 22(2), 284–309.

Walsh, G. S., Cunningham, J. A., Mordue, T., McLeay, F., O'Kane, C. and Connolly, N. 2021. What business schools do to support academic entrepreneurship: a systematic literature review and future research agenda. *Studies in Higher Education* 46(5), 988–999.

Walsh, K., Nelles, J. and Stephens, S. 2023. Recycling in entrepreneurial ecosystems: the phenomenon of boomeranging. *R&D Management* 53(4), 709–727.

Wang, F., Xia, J. and Xu, J. 2020. To upgrade or to relocate? Explaining heterogeneous responses of Chinese light manufacturing firms to rising labor costs. *China Economic Review* 60, 101333, 1–15.

Waters, R. and Lawton Smith, H. 2008. Social networks in high-technology local economies: the cases of Oxfordshire and Cambridgeshire. *European Urban and Regional Studies* 15(1), 21–37.

Wennberg, K., Wiklund, J. and Wright, M. 2011. The effectiveness of university knowledge spillovers: performance differences between university spinoffs and corporate spinoffs. *Research Policy* 40(8), 1128–1143.

Weterings, A. and Knoben, J. 2013. Footloose: an analysis of the drivers of firm relocations over different distances. *Papers in Regional Science* 92, 791–809.

Wright, M., Lockett, A., Clarysse, B. and Binks, M. 2006. University spin-out companies and venture capital. *Research Policy* 35(4), 481–501.

Wright, M., Piva, E., Mosey, S. and Lockett, A. 2009. Academic entrepreneurship and business schools. *Journal of Technology Transfer* 34(6), 560–587.

Wright, M., Siegel, D. S. and Mustar, P. 2017. An emerging ecosystem for student start-ups. *Journal of Technology Transfer* 42, 909–922.

Wurth, B., Stam, E. and Spigel, B. 2022. Toward an entrepreneurial ecosystem research program. *Entrepreneurship Theory and Practice* 46(3), 729–778.

Wynarczyk, P. and Raine, A. 2005. The performance of business incubators and their potential development in the North East Region of England. *Local Economy* 20(2), 205–220.

Xiao, H., Wu, A. and Kim, J. 2021. Commuting and innovation: are closer inventors more productive? *Journal of Urban Economics* 121, 103300, 1–16.

Yi, Y. 2018. Firm relocation and age-dependent reliance on agglomeration externalities. *Annals of Regional Science* 61, 439–456.

Zane, L. J. and DeCarolis, D. M. 2016. Social networks and the acquisition of resources by technology-based new ventures. *Journal of Small Business & Entrepreneurship* 28(3), 203–221.

Zawdie, G. 2010. Knowledge exchange and the Third Mission of universities. *Industry & Higher Education* 24(3), 151–155.

Index